DayTrading into the Millennium

Michael P. Turner

If you have any questions or comments about this book, you can e-mail the author at feedback@tradersresource.com.

For more information about related products and services, please visit the http://www.tradersresource.com website.

ISBN 0-9668602-0-9

Library of Congress cataloging of publication is in process.

This publication is designed to provide informative information in regard to the subject matter covered. It is sold with the understanding that the author and or publisher is not engaged in rendering legal, financial, accounting, or other professional services. If such expert assistance is required, the services of a competent professional person should be sought.

Printed in the United States of America.

TABLE OF CONTENTS

DEDICATION

I dedicate this book to my Grandfather, Emanuel R. Posnack. He passed away at the young age of 92, when I was sixteen years old. He was the author of several books on political theory and the economy, an engineer, an inventor, and most importantly, the most upstanding, honest, moral person that I have ever met.

He is my mentor and my idol. Without him, I would not be here today. He has given me inspiration in life and in death. I only wish he could be here today.

DayTrading into the Millennium

ACKNOWLEDGEMENTS

I would like to thank my family for all of the support that they have given me over the years. Although I was the one to pen this book, they all played a part in its creation, both genetically and spiritually.

I would like to thank David Stern. Achieving success by following his heart and not the almighty dollar was a lesson that he alone taught me, not through words, but through actions.

I would like to thank my professors at Lehigh University for the guidance and wealth of knowledge that they instilled in me and for their inspiration. They all contributed to this book in one form or another.

I would like to thank Bea Kallina for the support and inspiration she gave me to go after my dream. Had she not been there for me, I may have stayed where I was longer than I should have and not followed my heart at the time it told me to move to Manhattan.

I would like to thank Frank Murphy. Although he probably did not know how much I learned by observing his work at Lehman Brothers, he inspired me.

I would like to thank Tony Bruan, one of the best traders I have ever met. He probably did not know how much I learned by observing him at his hedge fund.

Nonetheless, he is truly an inspiration in my life.

I would like to thank the following friends for their support and companionship along the way: Desiree Bagheri, Susanna Blackburn (and family), Kristin Bruan, Alistair and Jennie Currie (and family), Smedley Ducker, Fiona Gallagher (and family), Hugo Isaac, Jason Kronick, Barbara O'Neill, Michael Spector (and family), Kira Stadele, Doug Weaver, Oliver and Laura Westmacott (and family), and the rest (they know who they are). Words do not describe the degree to which I cherish their friendship.

Finally, I would like to thank Amy Gensler for editing this book and David Lieberman for his contribution to the Listed Trading, Appendix A of this book.

INTRODUCTION

This book was written for a broad audience of investors and traders. For those who have little or no knowledge of the financial markets, some of the subjects covered may be difficult to understand. The book begins with the evolution of the DayTrading industry and provides some background for the reader. It then explains what I feel is the best way for a new DayTrader to get started, and examines the pros and cons that relate to brokers, trading platforms, training, and methods of trade entry and execution. The rest of the book includes detailed explanations of market activity and trading strategies.

When arranging the contents of the book, I made every attempt to progress in a format that builds upon earlier chapters. However, because of the inter-related nature of the topics discussed, some phrases, terms, and ideas are mentioned before they are fully defined. After completing this book, I believe you will have a solid understanding of every topic that I cover.

To fully grasp and implement the concepts and strategies detailed in this book, I suggest, after reading the book thoroughly, using it as a manual to assist you in your independent study.

Enjoy.

1 EVOLUTION OF THE DAYTRADING INDUSTRY

In 1971, the National Association of Securities Dealers (NASD) created a computerized over the counter equities market called the National Association of Securities Dealers Automated Quotation (Nasdaq). Unlike the New York Stock Exchange (NYSE) and the American Exchange (AMEX), Nasdaq is not a physical exchange. Nasdaq is a network of more than 5,000 dealers who are connected electronically. In 1985, the Small Order Execution System (SOES) was born under the penumbra of the Securities Exchange Commission (SEC) as a means of improving market efficiency. However, SOES did not become mandatory until after the crash of 1987. At that time it became almost impossible to reach overwhelmed dealers, many of whom "backed away" from the market. Shortly after the crash, the SEC made SOES mandatory to "ensure access to the market by the small investor." As an offshoot, this new policy enabled the birth of a new type of trader, the "SOES" trader, also known as "SOES Bandit."

In early 1989, Harvey Hautkin capitalized on market inefficiencies caused by SOES and opened the nation's first "retail" SOES shop in New Jersey. It was at this location that DayTraders implemented what is known today as SOES trading. Simply put, SOES trading is the art of "scalping" (which although not arbitrage in the truest sense of the term it was a close second).

In the early 1990s, spreads were wider, and there were very few SOES traders utilizing this strategy. With little or no experience or background in equity trading (or the financial markets in general), many SOES traders were making in excess of $1,000,000 per year with as little as $100,000 in trading capital. Fundamental and technical analysis were rarely used. The software used to monitor the markets was rudimentary and lacked decision support, risk management, and account management tools. Orders were shouted across the trading desk to order entry clerks who then entered orders into a Nasdaq workstation and verbally confirmed executions.

During this period, the NASD tried to put SOES Bandits out of business by lowering the number of shares that they could trade on the system to a maximum of 500 shares. After much legal battling and posturing, the limit was restored to a maximum of 1,000 shares. Quite recently, this limit was lowered to 100 shares.

How Scalping Worked...

SOES traders sought to identify volatile stocks displaying momentum characteristics (i.e., rapid price change) with either a strong upward or a strong downward bias. For stocks trading with a strong upward bias, for example, SOES traders could preference OTC market makers with a bid slightly above the "inside" bid price using Nasdaq's SelectNet execution system. If the SOES trader was willing to take the current offer price, he or she would usually use SOES for a mandatory execution of the trade. Depending upon where the buy order was filled, the trader would wait for the bid to uptick a bit, and would then "SOES" out of the trade for a profit ranging from 1/8 to 1/2 point. For stocks displaying a downward bias, the opposite would apply.

As more participants entered the SOES market, spreads began to narrow and competition for executions on both SelectNet and SOES increased. The maturing of the SOES market mimicked the maturing process that all other securities markets experienced when competition increased. For example, in the not too distant past, the U.S. Treasury Market had spreads as wide as 25 basis points or more. Today, the same market has spreads of two basis points or less. The Junk Bond Industry of the 1980s had spreads as wide as 1,000 basis points or more. Today's Junk Bond market averages far narrower spreads of 300 basis points or less. The REIT, Repo, Currency, Commodity, Futures, and Options markets have also undergone the same maturation process of increased competition and narrowed spreads over the years. In response to this increasingly competitive nature of the SOES marketplace, the antiquated market monitoring systems that SOES traders were using have been replaced by more sophisticated models.

Even with the introduction of high-end trading systems, SOES traders found that using the over the counter "scalping" strategy exclusively was not enough to maintain profit levels. New NASD rules were implemented which made it more difficult for SOES traders to take advantage of this new market. One such rule is the "five-minute rule," which prohibits multiple trades in the same stock within a five-minute period.

Given new rules and increased competition for eighths and quarters, traders were forced to broaden their scope of trading strategies to maintain profit levels. Today's successful DayTraders no longer concentrate exclusively on the Nasdaq over the counter market. The trading of listed stocks on an intraday basis has become an integral part of DayTraders' strategies, adding more than 3,000 stocks to the universe of more than 6,800 over the counter stocks. In addition, the most successful traders have implemented a "three tiered" approach to DayTrading (a combination of scalping, fundamental, and technical strategies). The "SOES Trader" of yesterday has been replaced by the "Equity DayTrader" of today. Table 1 shows a comparison between the Old "SOES Trader" and "Today's Equity DayTrader."

I have often been asked, "How would you describe the average or typical DayTrader?" The following is a summary of more than 1,000 conversations that I have had with DayTraders over the past year. Obviously, DayTraders have varied styles of trading, and no two DayTraders trade exactly alike. However, the following is a pretty accurate depiction of today's equity DayTrader.

Depending upon overall market trends and fluctuations, both on an intermediate (weekly and monthly) and short-term (hourly and daily) basis, different trading strategies must be used to realize and capitalize on price movements. From an intermediate perspective, the equity market (at the time this book was written) continues its relentless bullish trend. From a short-term perspective, today's market displays a

Table 1. Old "SOES Trader" vs. Today's "Equity DayTrader"

The Old "SOES Trader"	Today's "Equity DayTrader"
Operated in a relatively noncompetitive environment with a limited number of participants and wider spreads.	Operates in a highly competitive environment with narrow spreads.
Required little or no understanding of equity markets or other financial markets.	Requires substantial knowledge and understanding of the equity markets, as well as the interplay of the bond, futures, and overseas markets.
Required little training and offered "easy" profit opportunities.	Requires continuous research and homework to be successful and has a six-month or longer learning curve.
Nearly anyone could be a successful SOES trader.	Only intelligent, savvy, knowledge-able, disciplined DayTraders survive in today's environment.
Limited trading to Nasdaq over the counter equities.	Trades both listed and Nasdaq equities.
Used rudimentary software that lacked decision support, risk man- agement, and account management tools. Orders were shouted across the room to order entry clerks who then shouted back confirmations.	Used sophisticated, fully-integrated market monitoring and trade execution platforms that include decision support tools and filters, trade and account management systems, capital utilization and risk control tools, and sophisticated electronic execution functions complete with artificial intelligence routines. Order routing and confir- mation is completely electronic, with execution times as quick as 1/2 second.
Used only the "scalping" technique.	Utilizes a combination of scalping, fundamental, and technical analysis.
Traded only is SOES trading shops.	Trade in hedge funds and equity DayTrading shops as well as re-motely throughout the United States via Internet, direct dial-up, and frame relay connections.

pattern of highest volatility in the first hour of the trading day, followed by moderate to high volatility in the last 45 minutes of trading with relatively low volatility in between. In today's marketplace, volatility is not evenly distributed across all sectors or even individual stocks within sectors. Given this environment, traders often use the aforementioned "three tiered" approach to DayTrading.

By closely following historical and breaking news on different stocks and industry sectors, in combination with technical analysis, DayTraders can effectively capitalize on price inconsistencies and intraday swings in stock price. Using this combination strategy, DayTraders will (depending upon the time of day and the market conditions) seek out gains of 1/16 of a point up to 1 to 3 points or more. Given these market conditions, it is not uncommon for DayTraders to hold intraday positions for a number of hours. In the event that a DayTrader is seeking to capture strong intraday price movements, he/she will often withstand intraday "open position" losses of 1/2 to 3/4 of a point before abandoning the trade (versus the old strategy of exiting all trades with a loss of 1/8 to 1/4 of a point). By expanding the risk tolerance per trade, DayTraders position themselves to capture broader price movements without getting "shaken out" or "whipsawed" from positions.

2 THE PASS/FAIL RATE OF DAYTRADING

In my current position, I have the opportunity to speak with DayTraders from around the world on a daily basis. One of the most common questions both novice DayTraders and individuals considering DayTrading as a profession ask me is, "What is the success rate of DayTrading?"

If the year were 1989, my answer would be close to 100 percent. "SOES" trading was a new style of speculation at that time. The SOES market was "immature." Spreads were wide, competition was slim, and the potential to make huge profits was great. Experience and knowledge of the equities market or financial markets in general was not a prerequisite for this course. Grocery clerks, shoe salesmen, and auto mechanics alike signed on and began reaping large rewards almost from the outset.

If the year were 1994, my answer would be in the neighborhood of 75 percent. The SOES market at this time was picking up speed, and perking the interest of a sizeable number of people. Spreads were narrower and the field of play was becoming increasingly competitive. Still, at this point in time the market had not fully matured. Profit opportunities abound, and

"SOES Bandits" (many of which had little or no knowledge of the financial markets) were making money.

If the year were 1996, my answer would be around 50 percent. At this juncture, the game truly began to change. Before this point in time, traders would shout their orders over the trading desk to order entry clerks who would then enter the trades into a Nasdaq workstation. Once trades were executed, the clerks would then shout confirmations back to the traders. Traders were using simplistic market monitoring tools, devoid of decision support tools and containing primitive (or nonexistent) account and risk management systems. Profit opportunities were still abundant, and the trend of the market complemented this type of trading quite nicely. However, competition was everywhere and increasing rapidly, and the Darwinian rule of survival began to take a stand in the industry.

If the year were 1997, my answer would be 40 percent. The SOES industry was a household name by this point, and everyone and their cousin wanted to get in. SOES trading rooms were in most major cities throughout the United States, and remote dial-in and Internet based DayTrading systems became widely available. Competition was fierce and getting fiercer every day. Traders began relying more heavily on software, hardware, and networking technology to gain a competitive edge. Traders no longer had to shout orders to clerks and wait for verbal confirmations. Sophisticated decision support tools, account and risk management systems, trade execution features and methods were introduced, and traders (like sheep) migrated to the best systems available. Those who did not upgrade quickly found themselves at a competitive disadvantage, and began falling to the bottom of the DayTrading food chain.

Now, in the year 1999, my answer is 20 percent. Today's DayTrading industry is, in my humble opinion, one of the most difficult forms of speculation that any trader can engage in. Diligent research, patience, discipline, and understanding are required, and traders must be supported by the most sophisticated trading platform available. I will further refine the 20 percent success rate by saying that out of 100 people that take up DayTrading, 40 will fail in the first six months, 20 will fail in the following six months, and 20 will die off during the following year.

The truth is that this 20 percent survival rate is somewhat misleading. It is similar to saying that if a man has one foot in a fire and the other on a block of ice that he is, on average, comfortable. The reason that people fail at DayTrading is because they do not take this business seriously. They are not disciplined, dedicated, and patient. I estimate that 50 percent of those who fail at DayTrading could have been successful if they had the right attitude and approach. After removing this fifty percent from the picture, the survival rate is somewhere around 60 percent. The question then remains, "What is the fate of those who succeed at DayTrading?"

For those who survive, the picture is a Monet. Successful DayTraders are, in my opinion, the savviest traders around. They understand what makes the market work, how it works, and when it works. These traders, using 2-1 margin, realize annual returns ranging from 40 to 100 percent or more. They can profit in all market conditions and consistently make money. Their strategies are relatively low risk in comparison to the high returns that they realize. These traders have my utmost respect. If you are one of them, congratulations on a job well done. You and I both know that your success has little to do with luck.

After reading this, some readers probably wish they had kept their day jobs. For other readers, I believe there is a common question: "How do I become one of the few that survives?" Good question.

3 Is DayTrading Gambling?

When I first began DayTrading, I tried to explain to my grandmother, who is in her upper 80s, what I was doing. My grandmother is a social worker and has been (and still is) helping others work through various problems in their lives. She is a brilliant, vibrant woman, and mentally more together than most people half her age. She is a great listener and a person who knows how to ask all of the right questions.

I spent the better part of an hour explaining to her what I was doing. I explained how I timed my entry and exit points, and how I based my buy and sell decisions on intraday news events as well as the general movements of the market on an intraday basis. When I was finished she paused, lit a cigarette, took a big drag, and blew it toward the ceiling. She looked at me, took another drag, blew it in my general direction and said, "So, what you are doing is gambling." Of course I didn't like that. When put in those terms, it somewhat degrades what I consider to be a very regal profession. My immediate reaction was to defend my colleagues, the DayTrading industry, and myself...which I did vehemently.

I am somewhat of a stubborn person, and I think that I inherited this trait from my dear grandmother. We discussed (actually we argued) the point for a while, and eventually agreed to disagree, which we often do. (I'm sure that you will read this, Grandmother. After completing this chapter, you will see that I really do listen to what you have to say.)

After not winning but not losing this "discussion" with my grandmother, I began considering the difference between gambling and DayTrading. There is certainly risk associated with both, and luck and skill each play a part in both. So then, is DayTrading a form of gambling? My conclusion is: yes and no.

Consider a casino. You are sitting on one side of the blackjack table, and the dealer (the house) is on the other side of the table. Both you and the dealer are playing the same game, so is it true that you are both gambling? Yes and no. The yes part is obvious. The no part is somewhat subtler. Because the house has a statistical advantage over you, it will make money over time. While it is possible to win at blackjack, over time the average gambler will lose money. Gamblers that count cards can turn the odds in their favor, giving them a statistical advantage over the house. That's why casinos ask card counters to kindly leave and never return.

A statistical advantage of plus or minus five percent, depending upon how good the player is, gives the house enough of an advantage to pay for a hotel, staff, tables, the casino, parking, insurance, and advertising. With a slight but consistent statistical advantage, the house can make an inordinate amount of money. In my opinion, the answer to whether the house is TRULY gambling is clearly NO. The house is running a business with a statistical advantage.

There are "games" at casinos that are truly made for the sucker, like the wheel of money or the slot machines. Play the slots for long enough and I guarantee that you will lose all of your money. Sure, you may hit the jackpot, but if you continue to play, pure numerical statistics dictate that you will give all of your hard-earned money to the house. That's why the casinos have so many of them. Besides the action of putting the coin in the slot and pulling the lever (actually, you need only push the button now...more user-friendly), there is no human element involved, and no skill whatsoever.

DayTraders can, in essence, learn to count cards and beat the house. When a DayTrader develops the requisite skills, he or she becomes the house, rather than the gambler. Although each trade may result in a net gain or loss (as is the case at the blackjack table), over time a statistical advantage will yield a consistent return. The more tools a DayTrader has, the more he or she can shift the odds in his or her favor. When you have a statistical advantage you are no longer gambling, in my humble opinion. (So there, Grandma.)

If you do not have a statistical advantage, and you are guessing at price movements, then you truly are gambling. I understand that for some of you gambling is not legal in your state, and even if it were you could not gamble from the comfort of your own home. For those who have chosen DayTrading as a profession and are really just gambling, it is time to rethink your strategy.

DayTrading into the Millennium

4 IF I DECIDE TO DAYTRADE, HOW SHOULD I BEGIN?

The first piece of advice that I will offer to those who are contemplating a career as a DayTrader is:

"TAKE IT SLOW!"

Daytrading is a business. All businesses, regardless of the product or service being offered, have a startup period during which no revenue is generated. Careful research, planning, and preparation is required to get the business up and running. As the founder, chairman, CEO, and janitor of your DayTrading organization, you have a considerable amount of work to do.

First and foremost, you will need trading capital. To make a living DayTrading, you will need to determine the income that you need to generate (after taxes) to support your lifestyle. In the first year of trading, be conservative, and assume that you will make nothing. (As with any business venture, there is a distinct possibility that you are not cut out for this type of business and will not be successful.) In the second year, be conservative again, and plan on an annual return of 25 percent on your capital (or 50 percent if you are doubling your buying power with margin). Finally, you will have to add in the initial start-up cost of software, hardware, research materials, and supplies. Based on these variables, you can determine how much capital you will need to get your business up and running.

Let's assume that after taxes you will need $25,000 to support yourself for a year. Let's also assume that you have no equipment. Therefore, you will need a computer and printer ($3,000), as well as books, publications, and supplies ($2,000). So far, this adds up to $30,000.

Use the following formula to calculate the trading capital (C) necessary to support yourself for a year (S), after taxes (T), given a rate of return (R). Since most brokers do not charge interest on intraday margin, it is advantageous to use margin for DayTrading. The "2" in the following formula represents 2 to 1 margin. If you choose not to use margin, then remove the 2 from the formula.

$$\frac{S}{2R(I-T)} = C$$

Let's say that $25,000 is your annual income requirement (after taxes of 30 percent) to support yourself, and you expect to realize an annual return of 50 percent using margin in your second year of trading:

$$\frac{\$25,000}{(2 \times 0.5)(1 - 0.3)} = \$35,714$$

Based on this example, the total amount of capital that you will need to get your DayTrading business off the ground is roughly $66,000. If you do not have

$66,000 sitting in the bank, then you have two choices. Your first choice is to find an investor to back you. If you choose to go this route, you will need to add to the above equation the interest (i) that you will have to pay your backer for the loan (L):

$$\frac{(S + Li)}{2R(1-T)} = C$$

Because the interest that you will be paying on the borrowed funds will increase the overall trading capital that you will need to get started, the initial solution to the equation will need to be recalculated to account for interest.

For example, assume that you have $40,000 in the bank and need to borrow $26,000 at 18 percent interest:

$$\frac{[\$25,000 + (\$26,000 \times 0.18)]}{(2 \times 0.5)(1 - 0.3)} = \$42,400$$

Given a $26,000 loan at 18 percent interest, you will need trading capital of roughly $42,000. Therefore, you will need a total of $72,000, or a loan of $32,000. The next step is to plug this value into the formula and recalculate:

$$\frac{[\$25,000 + (\$32,000 \times 0.18)]}{(2 \times 0.5)(1 - 0.3)} = \$43,943$$

Regardless of the loan value and interest rate for the

loan, it will take two calculations to arrive at a rough value. The above example shows that you will need to borrow about $44,000 at 18 percent interest to satisfy your income requirements.

If you cannot borrow the necessary start-up capital, then your alternative is to DayTrade part-time or hold off on DayTrading altogether until you can afford to do so. I feel very strongly that DayTrading is a full-time job in itself, and I would urge anyone considering a part-time effort to reconsider. It is critically important for a DayTrader to be "in the market" full-time. If you do not pay constant attention to the market, I guarantee that you will miss out on crucial information that will inevitably cost you money — and perhaps a lot of it. This type of unnecessary risk is not a means to an end if your end is to DayTrade full-time. In fact, part-time DayTrading will likely result in a net loss of capital and leave you further from your goal than if you didn't DayTrade at all.

If you decide to hold off until you can afford to DayTrade full-time, set attainable goals for yourself. Decide how much you can afford to save each month and then figure out how long it will take you to achieve your goal. The time that it will take you to save enough start-up capital can be used to your advantage. Use this time to learn about trading and the actions of the market in general.

Regardless of whether you can or cannot afford to DayTrade full-time right away, I would suggest a similar "ramp-up" strategy (the only difference being the length of the ramp-up period). For those who are financially capable of entering into the DayTrading profession, I would suggest a ramp-up period of three months.

During this period there is a lot to do. The first step is to confirm that this is what you really want to do with your life. Begin researching the industry. The internet is by far the best place to learn about DayTrading. One of the best places to begin is at the Silicon Investor web site (http://www.techstocks.com). This site is a forum where investors and traders alike can post ideas, comments, and strategies. From this site, you will be able to obtain information about different books, periodicals, seminars, and brokers.

Begin watching the market. Make CNBC a part of your life. Subscribe to The Wall Street Journal, Investors Business Daily, and Barron's. I would not recommend subscribing to Forbes, Business Week, Money Magazine or any other financial publication, because the majority of the news in these magazines can be found in the Journal, IBD, or Barron's. I find that too many subscriptions makes for a lot of unread, wasted paper. It doesn't hurt to pick them up once in a while, and I always browse the covers at the local newsstand to see what the topic du jour is.

Assuming that your research confirms your desire to DayTrade for a living, the next step is to set a target start date for yourself. From a strategic planning standpoint, begin working on the projects that will take the longest to complete. The most complicated (and most important) project is finding the right broker and the right trading platform. Here you have two distinct choices. Either go to a DayTrading shop and trade from there, or trade from a remote location such as your home or office.

Don't assume that DayTrading shops are a better option because of on-site service and training. In my opinion, service and training are not components of physical location. "Virtual Trading Rooms" or "Chat Rooms" are common on the web. Using an interactive "Chat Channel," a number of organizations have created DayTrading forums, some of which have memberships in the thousands. The larger Virtual Trading Rooms and Chat Rooms are many times the size of the largest DayTrading shops. The main variable to consider is what value these forums add. How useful is the training? How does it compare to other outfits?

In the remote DayTrading industry, the broker and trading platform are one and the same. However, not all brokers and trading platforms are the same. In fact, there is a broad spectrum of brokers and services available. If you pick the wrong broker and trading platform, you may not be able to effectively implement your trading strategies. You may eventually fail as a DayTrader because of this alone.

Be very careful about whom you trust your money to. Not all organizations are the same. Some outfits are not broker dealers, but rather limited partnerships (some of which are very loosely regulated). Depending upon the partnership agreement, you may have little or no recourse in the event that the partnership goes out of business and does not refund your investment. Some brokers and clearing firms are grossly undercapitalized and may be financially insolvent. Even with SIPC insurance, if your broker or clearing firm goes out of business, your funds can be tied up for an extended period of time...which means that you will be out of business for an extended period of time. Well-capitalized, SIPC insured brokers and clearing firms that have additional cash bonding are the safest bet.

The key elements to consider are:

- Safety of your funds (is the broker [or the broker's clearing firm] adequately capitalized, SIPC insured, additionally cash bonded, etc.)
- Stability and reliability of the broker's software and execution system
- The functions and features of the trading platform itself
- Customer service, support, and training

Many of the on-line DayTrading brokers are experiencing reliability and stability issues. The reasons for this are fourfold.

First, the software platforms that many of the on-line DayTrading brokers are using are old technology. The programming code itself is often unstable. Many of these brokers license the software from other firms, and therefore they must rely on a third party to fix problems when they occur. This is time consuming, and the solutions (because they are idiosyncratic) are often merely temporary patches that eventually fail again.

Second is the networking and hardware configuration that these brokers have built. Fault tolerance and system redundancy is of paramount importance. Almost every week, I hear about a broker that has "gone down" for minutes or hours. We are not in the "Star Trek" era yet. Today's computers are subject to failure. (Even if we were in the Star Trek era, the Starship Enterprise experiences computer-related problems on virtually every journey.) The truth is that nothing in this world is perfect. Systems fail, tractors do dig through communications lines, satellites do get knocked out of alignment, and trees do fall on power lines from time to time. Therefore, the only way to build a "bomb proof" system is to incorporate redundancy throughout the system.

Even the most reliable broker, however, may not be your best bet. The type of execution system that the broker offers is one of the most crucial components of a complete system. A broker that offers a 100% reliable system but uses a web browser to route your order to its trading desk for execution is not compatible with DayTrading strategies. Orders are slow, confirmations are slow, and fills are poor. Because this piece of the puzzle is so important, I have dedicated the next chapter of the book to it (called "Methods of Execution").

Third are the connection options that these brokers offer to customers. For the most part, the Internet is the only option offered to traders. The Internet itself (as many of you already know) is often unstable and unpredictable. This is not to say that it does not work at all. In fact, depending upon the Internet Service Provider (ISP), the geographic area, and the method of connection (dial-up analog modem, ISDN, cable modem, ADSL, etc.) the Internet can be very stable and reliable most of the time. Keep in mind that even the most stable Internet connections can be slow or fail during times of high traffic. The only way to eliminate the shortcomings of the Internet is to not use it.

For those who are not fortunate enough to have a stable, reliable Internet connection, there are two alternatives — direct dial-up and dedicated connection. Direct dial-up connections are stable. Unfortunately, they are quite expensive, ranging from 5 to 15 cents per minute. In addition to the cost, direct dial-up connections have limited bandwidth, which reduces the amount of information that can be transmitted to the trader. The safest, fastest, most secure and reliable method of connection that you can use is a frame relay connection (also known as a fractional Tl). Personally, I would not connect any other way, regardless of the performance of my ISP. The reason for this is that when the market corrects (like it did at the end of October 1998), most ISPs either fail completely or are severely delayed. The Internet traffic caused by the 3 million on-line investors during that period was so heavy that the infrastructure of the Internet was completely overloaded. For those who had access to the markets on those days, the profit potential was huge. For those who did not have access on those days and could not exit their long positions, the losses were huge. In fact, given the feedback that I received from traders, the cost of a frame relay connection could have been paid for many years over from that one event.

Finally, the last cause of system instability and unreliability is overburdening of systems. The trend in the on-line DayTrading industry has been that of sheep and floodgates. When a new on-line DayTrading broker begins doing business, DayTraders (fed up with their current broker) flock like sheep to the new broker on the block. To accommodate these traders, the broker opens the floodgates and swamps its system with more cus-tomers than it can handle. This routine has been the norm during the past two years.

In terms of service, support, and training, there is a huge difference among the various on-line DayTrading broker dealers. If you call each broker that you are con-sidering, you will hear the same story: "We're the best!" The only way to evaluate this aspect is to ask around. Look on the Silicon Investor web site. Traders there are very vocal about their brokers and are not shy. There are some very blunt and revealing statements about brokers on this web site. Trust the testimonials of others. They are not salesmen and have no reason to lie about the service, support, reliability, and training that they have received from their broker.

With regard to training in particular, caveat emptor. Bad advice is worse than no advice at all, regardless of price. A $5,000 seminar that is poorly run and promotes outdated strategies that do not work in today's markets is a formula for disaster.

There are a number of brokers today who continue to teach the old "scalping" strategies. The reason for this is because scalping strategies generate the most transactions. In almost all cases today, a pure "scalper" will be unprofitable over time. The only party that will make money from this one-faceted trading strategy is the broker. I am not saying that all brokers are unscrupulous. This is not the case at all. In fact, a few brokers offer excellent trader training. What I am saying is beware! Once you have been to training, be careful what you do with the trading advice that you have been given. It is your capital at risk, not the trainers'. Backtest and paper trade their strategies before risking dime one. If you do decide to implement one of their strategies, start out small.

Once you have found the right broker, the next step is to open and fund the account. Depending upon the type of account and the funding method, this process can take anywhere from two days to three weeks. Writing out-of-state checks is a great way to delay the process by a week or more. If you are transferring cash, I suggest wiring your funds. This can be done from your bank or from another broker and is the fastest way to transfer funds.

Each broker will have different hardware requirements for their trading platforms. Therefore, it is wise to hold off on purchasing equipment until you know what your broker requires. In addition to computer hardware, you will also need to order the right connection. If you choose to use a dial-up analog modem, I recommend using a 56k modem, regardless of whether your ISP supports a connection at or close to that speed. In today's world (1999), the 56k modems are the newest, most advanced technology and will offer the highest degree of reliability. There are currently two types of 56k dial-up analog modems: the X2 and the Flex modem. It is important to first check with your ISP to see which type it supports.

ISDN and cable modems are faster and generally more reliable than dial-up analog modems. If you choose to use an ISDN or cable connection, the typical install time is about a week (although it can be considerably longer in some areas).

If you choose to use a frame relay connection, plan to wait four to six weeks to get your line installed. The monthly cost of a frame relay connection is about $350. If you are in a rural area (more than 10 miles outside of a town of 30,000 people or more), plan on paying considerably more for the frame connection.

While you are waiting for your account to be opened and funded, your hardware to be ordered and your line to be installed, begin diligently studying the markets. Buy a large three-ring binder, fill it with paper, and start taking notes. Paste articles from the different newspapers and magazines that you subscribe to in it. Highlight the key stories and take notes on what price movements you expect to result from the news. And yes, paper trade. Read more books on technical analysis, fundamentals, and trading strategies. Order annual reports from the companies that interest you. Immerse yourself, and prepare to open your doors for business.

Once everything is in place and you are feeling comfortable with your understanding of current market conditions, trading strategies, and your trading platform, it is time to start trading. Again, TAKE IT SLOW! Give yourself the luxury of time to learn and grow as a DayTrader. I guarantee that you will make mistakes when you begin trading. I guarantee that you will make very stupid mistakes as a novice trader. I guarantee that (if you are smart) you will learn from your mistakes and become a better trader. If you start off too aggressively, I guarantee you will make some very costly mistakes.

When you start trading, the plan should not be to make money, but rather to learn how to not lose money and to conserve your working capital. Trade in 100-share lots for the first two weeks. During this period I would be very surprised if you make money. In fact, there is a very high probability that you will lose money. Trading in 100-share lots it is almost impossible to make money DayTrading for eighths and quarters. When you trade in very small lots, commissions (which are typically $40 per round-trip trade) severely stack the odds against you. Assuming that you are successful in 50 percent of your trades, make 1/2 point on each of your successful trades, and only lose 1/4 of a point on your losing trades, you will lose $55 for every two trades that you make.

Plan on making five round-trip trades per day for the first two weeks. Consider it the cost of tuition. Given these parameters, you will lose $1,375 in your first two weeks of trading. In your second two weeks of trading, trade in 300-share lots. Expect to break even during this period. In the third two-week period, don't exceed 500 shares per trade, and then ease up from there as your comfort level increases.

The first three months are by far the hardest, and the vast majority of DayTraders are net losers of capital during this period. If you are net even after your first three months of DayTrading, you are doing great, and the future looks bright. Consider your lack of losses to be a scholarship and your losses to be the cost of tuition.

Regardless of your first-quarter results, don't get carried away. You are still a freshman in your first semester. If you are patient, diligent, and careful, you will stand a much better chance of success. Because you have set aside enough money to support yourself for a full year, there is no pressure to go after that extra buck. If you are pressured to trade in order to pay the rent, you are setting yourself up for disaster and should not be DayTrading.

I will conclude this chapter by re-emphasizing one point:

TAKE IT EASY!

Give yourself the luxury of time to stay in business. Carefully planning your strategy and treating DayTrading as a business is a required course. If you get off on the wrong foot or enter into this profession haphazardly, you will get eaten for lunch. The equities market is incredibly competitive and cutthroat. Other traders, market makers, and specialists are out to take your money, just as you are out to take theirs. In this industry you are either predator or prey. You decide.

Remember...

The reason that 80 percent of DayTraders fail is not because they get tired of DayTrading or miss their old job. These traders lose most of their trading capital and have no choice but to resign. DayTrading, as with any other form of investing, is risky. If you cannot afford to lose 100 percent of your trading capital, please (for your own sake) don't do this!

5 Methods of Execution

When choosing a broker, one of the key elements to consider is what execution methods are offered. A broker that offers the most technologically advanced software platform, is 100 percent stable and reliable, and has the best customer service on the planet is not nearly enough. A broker that uses a web browser to route customer orders to its trading desk for execution is slow, and the fills are often far less than desirable — not to mention that trade confirmations and cancellations of trades can often take many minutes. For DayTraders, direct access to the markets is crucial for success. Relying on a broker to route your orders for you is a formula for disaster. One of the primary reasons so many DayTraders fail in the first six months is because of the execution platform they are using to implement their trading strategies. Poor, slow fills not only cost DayTraders money, but they eliminate many trading strategies from the realm of possibility.

There are a handful of on-line DayTrading brokers today that offer direct access to the markets. Direct access to the markets allows traders to route their orders through their broker's back office and on to the exchanges. For Nasdaq over the counter trading, there are a number of different execution methods. The most popular are SelectNet (SNET), the Small Order Execution System (SOES), and Electronic Communication Networks called ECNs (the most popular of which are Terra Nova [TNTO], Island [ISLD], and Instinet [INCA]). For listed trading, the SuperDot system is used to route orders directly to the specialists' posts on the floor of the exchanges. Each execution system has its advantages and disadvantages, but all are superior to using a web browser to route orders to a broker's trading desk.

When using direct access to the exchanges, there are various order routing and execution rules that the trader must follow. Before you begin trading using direct access, it is crucial that you fully understand all of these rules as well as the pros, cons, and idiosyncrasies of each of these systems. Because these rules are subject to frequent change, always check with your broker for the most recent rules, policies, and guidelines. If you think that you can learn as you go, you can. However, the cost of tuition may be greater than five Club Med vacations. (Trust me on this one.)

SNET

In the Nasdaq over the counter market, there are a number of ways to execute a trade. I will begin with Nasdaq's execution systems, SNET and SOES. SNET is a way for traders to send orders to market makers or ECNs. Traders can either "preference" a single market maker or ECN or "broadcast" to an entire level of market makers. When "broadcasting" to market makers via SNET, there is no preset time limit in which market makers must respond. When "preferencing" a market maker via SNET, the market maker has 15 seconds to accept or decline the order. In either case, traders must wait 10 seconds before canceling an SNET order. When preferencing an ECN, the execution is not automatic. The ECN has 10 seconds to accept or decline an order. For traders who can access ECNs directly, order execution is automatic (if the trader is "first in line" and there is a counter-party at the same price).

Some market makers are notorious for walking away from or not honoring the shares that they are offering. Some are slow to respond to you. Others, like Goldman Sachs (GSCO), Merrill Lynch (MLCO), and Morgan Stanley & Co. (MSCO), are generally good about honoring or rejecting trades quickly. Depending upon the security being traded and the market conditions, some market makers are better to deal with than others. Only experience will reveal who these market makers are.

The only disadvantage associated with the SNET method of execution is that it is not mandatory. The advantage to the trader is that he or she can effectively step around a "herd" of traders attempting to execute trades at the market. For example, a trader who is long stock can do this by offering stock below the inside bid, effectively crossing the market to get out of a long position that is quickly running to the downside. The trader can also bid for stock above the inside ask for an equal but opposite result. When market makers get preferenced outside of the inside market, they are more inclined to fill the order because it is arbitragable. The market maker can buy shares from you below the bid and sell them at the inside bid immediately, or sell stock to you above the ask and immediately buy them back at the inside ask.

Although you are forfeiting 1/16 or 1/8 by going outside of the inside market to open or close a trade using SNET, you have a much greater chance of getting filled. In all likelihood, if you attempt to enter or exit a trade at the inside market when it is running against you, you will be queuing behind a large number of traders attempting to do the same thing. In all likelihood, you will get a worse fill than if you sucked it up and gave away a teenie (1/16) or an eighth to exit the trade outside of the market. Don't be cheap — be smart.

For stocks exhibiting a great deal of momentum or "velocity," using this method of execution is quite effective. If you feel that a particular stock is going to run considerably, don't be afraid to pay a little more to get in. My uncle (who has been trading for many decades) always told me that, when trading options, "If I like the trade, I like it!" A sixteenth or an eighth makes little difference in a trade that I am seeking a dollar or more from. This also holds true in DayTrading. If you are looking for as little as a quarter, and you think the bid price is going to go up at least 3/8 of a point from its current level, don't be afraid to get in at a higher price. It is better than missing the trade altogether.

Remember...

When a stock is running, a market order will often give you a worse fill than if you just sucked it up and took the stock at a price just outside of the market to begin with.

SOES

SOES is a mandatory execution system. This means that a market maker bidding for or offering stock at the inside quote is obligated to honor the trade, and the execution of that trade is mandatory. The advantage is obvious.

There are some huge disadvantages to using SOES. The first is that the maximum number of shares that can be executed over SOES is 100. Second, once you buy (or sell) on SOES you cannot buy (sell) that same stock again for five minutes. (You can exit the trade using SOES within five minutes, but you cannot add another trade on the same side during this period.) Additionally, if you buy (or sell) on SOES, you cannot buy (sell) on SNET or any ECN for the remainder of that five-minute period. This is known as the five-minute rule.

The third disadvantage is that a SOES order is at the inside market. When a stock is running, there are many market participants queuing to execute trades on SOES. Therefore, you must stand in line. This can be extremely costly, and stocks will sometimes run through many levels before you get executed on SOES.

The final disadvantage of using SOES is that you cannot SOES an ECN. When an ECN comes to the inside bid or ask while you have an order outstanding, it is automatically rejected and you cannot re-enter the SOES order until the ECN leaves the inside quote. If you were first in line to be executed before the ECN showed up, you would lose your place in line and have to queue again after the ECN leaves. Expected in 1999, Nasdaq will be implementing a policy that will allow a trader using SOES to remain in queue for 90 seconds when an ECN comes to the inside market. In the meantime traders are stuck with this disadvantage. SOES is most effective in calm stocks. When the stock is stagnating, a SOES order is one of the quickest, most reliable ways to execute small trades.

ECNs

ECNs have become an integral part of over the counter executions in recent years, and account for roughly 25 percent of all Nasdaq executions today. Instinet (INCA) is the most widely used of all ECNs and is only offered directly to institutions and high net worth individuals. However, using SNET, a trader can preference an INCA order and take advantage of the liquidity that INCA provides in the marketplace without having direct access to it. The only disadvantage of using INCA is the cost. In addition to the transaction cost that brokers charge traders, Instinet charges about 1.5 cents per share. With as little as a sixteenth improvement in price, it is beneficial to take advantage of INCA.

Island is by far the most widely used "retail" ECN (Instinet is considered to be an "institutional" ECN) and is a tool that one cannot afford to do without. ISLD is very liquid, and executions are lightning quick in the most actively traded stocks. ISLD allows retail investors to essentially "make markets." For example, if the market in SAPE is 45 1/2 bid for 1,000 shares, 1,000 shares offered at 45 3/4, a trader who wants to go long the stock (but does not want to take the offer) can bid for 1000 shares on ISLD at a price of 45 9/16. Typically in less than a second, the trader's order is represented on the Level II screen as ISLD. Because the trader's bid is the highest available bid, he or she has the highest probability of getting filled at that price. As soon as the trader is filled, he or she can turn around and offer the stock at 45 11/16, for a quick scalp of an eighth.

One disadvantage of using ISLD is that partial fills are very common. If you use ISLD for a week, I can all but guarantee that you will get some very odd fills (like 14 shares, 92 shares, or 327 shares). Although this can be annoying, you do not have to re-enter your order. You keep your place at the front of the line until your order is completely filled. If your broker dealer does not offer direct access to ISLD, you can (as with Instinet) preference outstanding orders using SNET. This works. However, if your broker does not offer direct access to ISLD, I STRONGLY recommend that you find a broker who does. ISLD is an incredibly powerful tool and one that the DayTrader cannot afford to go without.

There is also Terra Nova (TNTO). Terra Nova is similar to ISLD, but is far less liquid. Therefore, fills are slower and sometimes nonexistent. If your broker does not have direct access to TNTO, you can still preference TNTO via SNET. Having both is just that much more advantageous.

There are a number of new ECNs, such as Attain (ATTN), Bloomberg (BTRD) and Spear Leeds & Kellogg (REDI). They are reasonably new, so the liquidity of these ECNs is still in question. However, as time goes on, I believe that they too will become valuable tools for the DayTrader.

SuperDot

Unlike Nasdaq over the counter trading, listed trading follows a very different set of rules. To effectively trade the listed markets, a thorough understanding of both the types and methods of execution as well as the rules associated with them is necessary. Executions of listed trades (even over the SuperDot) are generally slower than Nasdaq over the counter trades. The reason for this is that a human being is calling out all orders to the "crowd" of brokers on the floor before actually pairing them off. This takes time. It is not to say that fills will be less than desirable on listed trades. Quite to the contrary — because of the specific rules surrounding the order in which trades are filled, you will get the best fills possible (in the absence of having your own floor broker) using the SuperDot system.

The SuperDot system is not an execution system, but rather an order routing system. (The "Dot" in SuperDot is an acronym for Designated Order Turnaround). Instead of calling your broker, who then calls his clerk who is stationed at a floor booth on the exchange floor, who then pages his floor broker, who then walks over to the post to execute the trade with the specialist, who then transmits the execution back to the clerk, who then contacts your broker and tells him the execution, who then notifies you — the SuperDot is a way to electronically transmit your order directly to the specialist, who can then electronically transmit your execution directly back to you. This description is a very simplistic rendition of listed trading. Appendix A provides detailed descriptions of the different trading rules, patterns, and idiosyncrasies of listed trading.

Just as E* Schwab, E* Trade and the other on-line brokers were the next generation of trade execution systems a few years ago, direct access to the markets is unquestionably the key to the next generation of trade execution systems today, and will remain so going into the next millennium. If you are a professional DayTrader and do not have direct access to the exchanges, you will either be a net loser of capital. If you are making money without direct access, you could be making more — and you are currently leaving a lot on the table.

I recommend to anyone who is considering using direct access to the exchanges to find a broker that offers hands-on training. I also recommend finding a system that offers a "trade simulator" or a system that allows you to electronically "paper trade" in real-time without risking capital. As I said before, it is critically important that you know the different order handling and execution rules COLD before you begin risking capital using direct access. If you are currently using an online broker, or have used one in the past, your broker has been doing for you what you can now do for yourself. And, as the old saying goes, "If you want something done right, do it yourself!"

6 GOING SHORT

Since the introduction of the SOES Bandit in the late 80s, the U.S. equities market has been bullish. In the past decade, the Dow Jones Industrial Average has nearly tripled in value. Anyone with money could have bought into index funds in 1989 and realized substantial returns over the past decade.

Many DayTraders have never experienced a bear market and have limited short-selling skills. Going long is the only strategy they know. This is dangerous and is a formula for disaster. Not "if" but "when" the market turns bearish, traders that are not skilled short-sellers will be out of business. Sure, there will be stocks that "fade the trend" during a bear market, but the opportunities to make a living as a DayTrader will be dramatically reduced.

Just as there will be opportunities to make money on the long side in a bear market, there are opportunities to make money on the short side in a bull market. By being able to go both long and short in all market conditions, you effectively double your trading opportunities and can significantly mitigate overall market risk. Regardless of whether the market is bullish, bearish, or neutral, there will be stocks to trade on both the long and short side.

Because of the uptick rule, getting short is harder to do than going long. When you find a short opportunity that is available through your broker, you will need to anticipate the top and get in early. Many times you will wind up getting short before the top, and will have to withstand larger movements against your entry point in order to capitalize on the anticipated movement. You should pick a maximum loss that you are willing to withstand before calling it quits and exiting the position. As a rule of thumb, this level should be greater than the maximum loss that you are willing to withstand in long positions, given the nature of short selling.

Another aspect of short selling that you will have to consider is sizing into the trade. Although it is possible to add to the position during upticks, this is difficult to do in many cases. However, given the added risk that you often take on in short trades, you might consider taking on smaller positions at the outset and adding to your position later (if possible).

The added advantage of shorting stock is that downside movements are often larger and faster than upside movements. I have made just as much money on the short side as I have on the long side, even in this tremendous bull market. Perhaps this is because I had a knack for picking out "dog stocks" (with fleas). It was easier for me to "see" overvalued stocks than undervalued stocks.

The primary tool that I use to evaluate the relative value of stocks is the Price Earnings (PE) Ratio. The PE Ratio measures the relationship between the share price and total company profits, which equals dividends plus retained earnings. The PE Ratio is an excellent tool to compare different companies. It is unbiased "relative" weight of the ratio of current stock price to earnings per share for different companies. Depending upon the sector that a company is in and the outlook that market participants have for that company, the PE Ratio will vary relative to other companies. The formula for calculating the current PE Ratio is:

$$PE = \frac{\text{current share price}}{\text{current earnings per share}}$$

Therefore, if the current stock price is $32, and a company's earnings per share equal $1.25, then the current PE Ratio equals 25.6.[1]

PE Ratios can also be calculated by substituting expected future earnings per share in the place of "current earnings per share." Regardless of whether you are comparing current or future expected PE Ratios, it is an excellent tool to compare the relative value of stocks in a given sector or broad market average. Stocks with the highest PE Ratios stand the greatest risk of sharp downside movements when very bearish news is released. Stocks with the lowest PE Ratios have the greatest propensity for sizeable upside movements when very bullish news is released.

A company like Network Solutions (NSOL), which has sported a PE Ratio of 200 or more, is a perfect example. This stock was grossly overvalued and corrected sharply when market participants turned against it. If you pay close attention to the most overvalued stocks, you will be in a good position to act when the time is right.

There are thousands of low PE stocks. It is far more difficult to single out stocks with single-digit PE Ratios, simply because there are so many of them. My advice would be to identify stocks with a PE Ratio of 75 or more, and pay the closest attention to stocks that have PE Ratios averaging 40 percent or more above the rest of the sector or broad market.

7 MONEY AND RISK MANAGEMENT

In every business, regardless of the product or service being offered, cash is king. The best idea with no money to bring it to market remains nothing more than an idea. Without money, there is no business. As a DayTrading business owner, you must always remember this and manage your cash carefully.

As a DayTrader, you will have many decisions to make over the course of days, weeks, and months. Active DayTraders will be making hundreds of money management decisions per week. Money management is not limited to buy and sell decisions. Money management includes decisions to not buy and to not sell. It also includes hardware purchases, subscriptions, network connections, cash withdrawals, and deposits. It includes the opportunity cost of deciding to allocate your working capital to one trade, rather than to another.

The bottom line goal of a DayTrader is not to learn more about the securities industry, become a better trader, or to be a better person. The bottom line of DayTrading is to make money — and as much as possible while maintaining a tolerable risk level. As a trader, you must constantly evaluate the risk/reward potential of every trade and weigh it against other trading opportunities.

In some cases, a piece of news will come out that affects an entire sector. In this instance, a choice must be made as to which security in the sector to trade and when to trade it. There are three primary variables to consider when deciding to enter a trade in order to optimize your trading solution.

The first variable is to decide which stock to trade and for what reason. This routine is going on all day as you scan the market for different opportunities.

Second is timing. Timing is everything. Ask yourself, "When and for what time period will I be in this trade?" Decide what the key elements of your timing decisions will be (both entry and exit) before you enter the trade, and stick to them.

How to enter and exit the trade is the third variable. How many shares should I start off with? What is my plan? Will I add to the position if it looks as though the trend will continue, or am I looking for a quick profit? What is the maximum loss that I am willing to take in the trade?

If you start off with a smaller share size, a larger negative price movement in the stock can be tolerated (given the total dollar loss tolerance that you have set for yourself). This will allow you greater "leeway" to compensate for lack of clarity on the timing issue.

For example, let's say that you are 80 percent certain that a stock will end the day higher than its current level, but you are unsure when and how it will get there. In this case, you might consider using a smaller share size to enter the trade. By doing this, the price movement in the stock (should it go against you initially) can be tolerated given your maximum capital loss tolerance for the trade.

However, be very careful when staying in losing positions. If a trade does not do what you thought it was going to do in the time frame that you thought it would do it in when you entered the trade, then what are you doing? Gambling? The only time that I would recommend sitting in a trade that goes against you initially is if you had made a determination like the one that I just described. You know the trade is there, you don't want to miss it, but you are unsure as to when and how it is going to get there. Great. If your capital risk tolerance complements the trade, do it. If the price goes down, and then clearly takes a turn to the positive side, and you are 80 percent certain that the movement is going to happen NOW, add to the trade. If you are wrong, liquidate the entire position and move on. Sometimes your mindset is not consistent with the rest of the market, and you are bound to lose. Don't get depressed over it. Just let it go and move on.

Sometimes it is not possible to determine every aspect of the "how" variable before the trade. Share size (as an indication of how sure you are about the trade) is an excellent money management tool. Sometimes you will find an opportunity that looks good enough to trade, but not good enough to tie up all of your capital on. In this case (in the absence of a better opportunity), make the trade, but cut the initial share size down. All great traders vary the size of their trades. In the DayTrading industry it is the norm to trade in 1,000-share lots. This phenomenon probably has something to do with the fact that if DayTraders trade 1,000-shares, it is easier for them calculate the P&L in their heads. If this is the only reason you trade in 1,000-share lots, bad idea!

Think of the number of shares traded in terms of

percentages. If you normally traded 1,000-share lots in the past, use that as 80 percent. Trade 1,000-shares if you are 80 percent confident that the trade will work. Trade 800 shares if you are 70 percent confident that the trade will work. Trade 500 shares if you are only 60 percent confident that the trade will work. Sometimes you will see a trading opportunity that looks good, but you aren't completely sure about the outcome. You are confident enough to risk some capital on the trade, but not confident enough to bet the farm. Don't. Use your money management skills to help determine the right size for the trade.

Another aspect to bear in mind, with respect to share size, is the type of trade you are considering. If you are thinking about taking an eighth out of a trade, don't consider less than 1,000 shares or $125 profit potential (unless you are in the "training" phase of your DayTrading career). An eighth on 500 shares is $62.50. After commissions, it doesn't even equal the price of a juicy steak at Harry's on Hanover (Manhattan prices). In a market where trading opportunities are plentiful and trading capital is limited, consider using smaller share sizes for "longer" term trades. If you feel that a stock is going to gain a point in the next five hours, but you know that there are plenty of other trading opportunities on that given day, consider buying 500 shares and sitting on them while you use the rest of your capital to take advantage of other opportunities.

Think statistically about trading for a moment. If you flip a coin and bet $100 on every toss, you will break even over time. If it costs you $10 to flip the coin each time, you will obviously be a net loser of capital. In terms of trading, if you make $100 half of the time and lose $100 half of the time, you will be a net loser of capital, given the cost of commissions. Therefore, you will need to either win more times than you lose or make more money on the winning trades than you lose on the losing trades. In truth, most short-term traders have less than a 50/50 success to loss ratio. Some of the better traders that I know make money on only 30 percent of their trades, but when they make money they make a lot of it.

If you scalp for a living, you will need to have a high success rate. In many market conditions, especially in the first and last hour of trading each day, scalping is a relatively easy way to make money. (I'm sure some would disagree with me on this point.) With the cost of commissions at roughly $40 per round trip trade and the average gross profit per trade at $125, any sizeable losing position will really hurt your bottom line.

Most traders have multiple trading strategies. Many scalp more aggressively in the morning and afternoon, look for larger gains during the hours in between, and still taking advantage of scalping opportunities when they present themselves. Whatever strategy you choose to employ, the key is to not lose money. Regardless of whether you are scalping or taking on long-term positions during the day, always keep your losses to a minimum. If you are seeking larger dollar gains, then you may have to withstand a larger downside capital risk to achieve these gains. However, there should always be a predetermined point at which you exit the trade and cut your losses, regardless of the extenuating circumstances (i.e., rationales).

Relative risk is one more aspect of money management that I would like to expand on. Some trades are far riskier than others, yet the profit potential is about the same. For example, trading GE during a smooth, upward-trending market is a relatively safe trade that I have often participated in. On the other band, trading CMGI on the same day could yield the same profit. However, when comparing CMGI to GE, the volatility and risk is much greater. Weighing relative risk is a key component of opportunity cost. Relative risk and opportunity cost are so closely related that it is impossible to separate the two. Always keep opportunity cost versus relative risk in the front of your mind when making your trading decisions.

The combinations of what to trade, when to trade it, and how to trade it are limitless. At first, it will be difficult to evaluate the relative risk and opportunity cost of trading. Over time, it will become second nature. If you are a novice trader, I suggest mastering this aspect of trading first. A great friend of mine once told me that once you learn how to NOT lose money, making money is simple. This is one of the most valuable insights anyone has ever shared with me.

If you can consistently NOT lose money, over time you will make money. The market is trending more times than not, which gives you a bias as to whether to go long or short. A trending market is similar to being able to see your first card at the blackjack table before making a bet. You have an edge from the outset.

If you have enough discipline, you can take advantage of the edge that the market presents to you. Over time, the market will present excellent trading opportunities. With more than 10,000 stocks to trade each day, opportunities are always available. It is simply a function of finding them and capitalizing on the best ones. Piece of cake, right?!

8 TIMING... ADD TO THE WINNERS, AND DITCH THE LOSERS

When entering a trade, please dispel the myth that you are buying based on the fundamentals of that particular stock. You are not investing for the long-term, you are DayTrading. While it is true that some stocks will increase 1,000 fold in the next 20 years, you are not buying for the next 20 years. You are buying for the next 20 minutes, or the next two hours. Fundamentals may have been the catalyst that alerted you to the opportunity, but timing is the key to DayTrading. There have been thousands of instances over the past three years when you could have bought Microsoft (a great company, with an incredible upward bias and a great outlook for the future) and still lost money...and a lot of it! When entering a DayTrade, the only variable that plays into whether a trade is profitable or unprofitable is timing.

If you pick the right time to enter and exit a trade, whether the strategy is on the long or short side, you can make money in almost any stock. If you pick the wrong time, you can certainly lose money in ANY stock. Therefore, when you enter a trade, you should predict that there will be a price movement that will occur within a predetermined period of time (beginning at the moment you enter the trade). You enter the trade to secure a position that will enable you to capitalize on this movement (should it occur). If the movement does not occur during the predetermined time frame, you must re-evaluate your position.

For simplicity, I will use long positions for the next few paragraphs, although the same rule applies for shorts. (Note that adding to short positions is sometimes very difficult, given the uptick rule.)

When re-evaluating your position, ask yourself, "Did the sector or broad market retrace since I entered the trade? Did the stock that I am trading show resistance to the trend of the market? If the market turns, will the stock complete the move that I initially anticipated when I entered the trade? Has my reason for entering the trade been proven valid? Invalid?"

If the stock that you are trading has declined in value, then you have taken a loss in that trade. Don't fool yourself by thinking that because you have not sold the stock you have not lost any money. This is wrong... very, very wrong. It is sometimes easier to frame this concept by saying to yourself, "I have already exited this trade at a loss of $X. Do I like the stock at this level? Would I buy the stock at this level here and now, or would I pass on the trade?" If the answer is "Yes, I like the stock at this level," then buy the stock. (You don't actually buy more shares, because you already own them. You just don't sell them.) If your answer is "No, I don't like the stock at this level, and I will pass on the trade," then don't buy the stock. (Since you are already long the stock, you need to exit the trade and move on.)

Some people like to use the term "dollar cost averaging." This is the process of adding to a position as it declines so that the average dollar cost of the total shares owned is lower than the share price of the initial trade. There are a few instances when I recommend that DayTraders do this. However, the vast majority of the strategies where I would employ dollar cost averaging are not DayTrades. For strict DayTraders that go flat every night, I consider dollar cost averaging to be "dumb" cost averaging in MOST cases. It is not to say that you should not employ this as an effective tool. Just be sure that when you do use it, it is for the right reasons. For the most part, if a trade does not complete the price action that you anticipated in the time frame that you anticipated, the time to add to the position is not now.

If the stock does not move at all, or moves marginally, re-evaluate the position in the same manner that you would a losing position. Be careful to resist adding to the position even if you feel very strongly that it is about to break out to the upside. You already bought it at that level...only you were a bit premature in your buying decision. If the price DOES begin to go up, consider adding to the position if you are confident that the trend will continue for a half point or more.

On the other hand, if the stock that you purchased moves in the direction that you thought it would, and you believe that the trend will continue, don't be afraid to add to the position. One indication that you may want to add to the position is that you are not selling the stock at its new higher price. Since you have already locked in a gain in the position, the risk of losing money on the trade is mitigated to some degree (even though you have not liquidated the position, the gain is yours...you can get out at the bid whenever you want). If the stock is trending upward and is in sync with the market, consider adding to the position. Remember, the trend is your friend.

When exiting a trade, many traders make the decision to either liquidate the entire position or stay in the entire position. Many DayTraders do not scale out of trades — they think in terms of black or white, with no shades of gray. One of the reasons that DayTraders do not average out of trades is because this strategy results in higher commission costs.

This is a ridiculous notion. If a transaction costs $20, and a 1/8 point move on 500 shares is $62.50, spend the $20 to potentially save the $62.50. If you are a "shade of gray" on a particular position, reduce your exposure. Think to yourself, "Do I like this particular stock at this particular price, at this particular time, with these particular market conditions?" If the answer is not a resounding "YES," but is somewhere above indifferent, then adjust your long position accordingly. You can always add back to the position later. If at any point during a trade you are not as bullish on the trade as you were when you entered it, reduce your position accordingly.

Never consider commission costs as part of a trade. If you are worried about $20, when you are risking $50,000, $500,000, or whatever your account size is, you are crazy. Don't base a buying or selling decision that is close to the value of your house on the price of a good Filet Mignon. Put it this way — if the basis of your trade ever comes down to commission costs, get out immediately and move on.

9 THE S&P FUTURES

If you were to ask 100 experienced DayTraders what the most valuable broad-market forecasting tool is, almost all of them would tell you that it is the S&P Futures contract. This chapter will define the contract, how it is calculated, and how it can be effectively used as a forecasting tool.

The S&P 500 Index is a capitalization-weighted index (each stock's market price is multiplied by the total number of outstanding shares in that company) with an aggregate market value of approximately 80 percent of the value of all NYSE listed securities. When originally created, a base index was created with a value of 100. The current index price is derived by comparing the current market value of all firms in the index with that of the base period. The S&P 500 Futures Index is a commodity contract that is based on the S&P 500 cash index.

The S&P Futures Index represents the "obligation to deliver" the value of the index on a certain future date (the expiration date). Only four futures contracts are traded. These contracts expire in March, June, September, and December. The most frequently traded contract is the nearest to expiration because it carries the smallest premium.

The symbols for these contracts are:

March... SPH9   September...SPU9
June......SPM9   December... SPZ9

Billions of dollars are traded each week based on the fluctuating premium of the futures versus the cash value. Fair value is the price at which investors are indifferent between buying stocks or buying futures. In other words, the "value" is the same, or "fair." If the futures contract becomes overvalued in comparison to the cash index, arbitrageurs will simultaneously sell the futures contract and buy the cash index (a portfolio of all or the majority of the stocks in the S&P 500 Index) to lock in a riskless profit. If the futures contract becomes undervalued in comparison to the cash index, arbitrageurs will do the opposite. When overvalued or undervalued conditions present themselves, arbitrageurs initiate what is called "program trading," which automatically "executes" the routines that I have just described. Program trades are typically gigantic and often cause sharp price movements when initiated. For DayTraders who understand how this aspect of the market works, significant DayTrading opportunities exist.

Because of the relatively high transaction costs associated with equities trading in comparison to futures trading, many institutional traders will hedge, rather than lighten up, their outstanding equities positions by selling the futures contract as insurance against depreciation of the equities position. Because traders do this, the futures index will react more quickly than the cash market. This is why so many traders use the futures as a leading indicator of stock movements. For example, when bearish traders begin selling futures contracts, the futures premium will drop. Depending upon current market sentiment, the premium that is accepted as "fair value" will fluctuate. However, if the futures premium drops too much, arbitrageurs will initiate program trades to capitalize on the imbalance, bringing the market back into sync.

When traders are bullish on the market, they will do the opposite and buy the futures contract to position themselves to realize enhanced returns from both the cash and the futures market. This will drive the futures premium up. Again, if the futures premium gets too far out of sync with the cash market (typically 75 basis points), arbitrageurs will step in and do their job. The transaction cost associated with program trading explains why most arbitrageurs will not initiate program trading until the premium gets out of sync by roughly 75 basis points.

As a forecasting tool, many traders analyze closing premiums to predict when major market moves will occur. As a rule of thumb, relatively large premiums (over four to five days or more) reflect market bullishness and are viewed as an indication of an upside breakout. Inversely, consistently low premiums are a bearish indicator. Because premiums decay over time and will equal zero at expiration (when the futures contract equals the cash index), a downward slope in premium is normal over time. When the futures contract gets within three weeks of expiration, the premium is so small that it becomes a relatively uninformative forecasting tool. At this point most traders will begin looking to the next contract for "advice."

There are two factors to consider when evaluating the S&P Futures contract and the relationship between the futures contract ("futures") and the S&P 500 Index ("cash"). First is the spread between the futures and the cash. In almost all cases, the futures will trade at a value above the cash. This is called "trading at a premium." In the rare instance that the futures trade at a value below the cash, it is called "trading at a discount." To calculate the premium (discount), subtract the cash value of the S&P 500 Index from the value of the S&P Futures contract.

Here is an example:

S&P Futures: 1280
S&P 500 (cash):   1278

In this example the spread, or premium, is 2.00.

Once you know the premium, the next step is to determine the fair value. The formula for fair value is as follows:

$$FV = (C \times [I-D])(X / 360)$$

C = The spot index price of the S&P Futures contract
i = Interest expense
D = Dividend income derived from the stock owned
X = Days remaining until expiration of the futures contract

Now that you understand how, why, and when program trading occurs, it is time to put this knowledge to work. Let's use the following information in the next example.

C = 1280
i = 7% (the annualized interest rate on a six-month T-Bill)
D = 5% (the average annualized dividend rate for the stocks in the S&P 500 Index, assuming a normal distribution of dividends throughout the year)
X = 75 (days to the expiration of the futures contract)

Therefore, the "fair value" premium for an S&P Futures contract with 75 days to expiration is as follows:

FV = 1280 x (.07 - .05) x (75 / 360)
FV = 5.33

Because the premium is 2.00, and fair value is 5.33, an imbalance exists between the futures and cash. In terms of fair value, the futures are under priced in relation to the cash. Therefore, arbitrageurs would likely initiate sell programs wherein the cash would be sold and the futures would be bought until fair value of roughly 5.33 is achieved.

By closely monitoring the premium of the futures contract in relation to fair value, you can effectively predict when buy and sell programs are going to be initiated. Because program trading causes dramatic, short-lived fluctuations in the market, a telltale indicator that a program trade has been initiated is the "Tick" indicator (a Base Zero indicator, explained in the next chapter). When the premium is close to the calculated level of program trading, and the Ticks spike up or down abruptly by 200-300 points or more, it is a strong indication that program trading was initiated.

If you are in a trade when program trading is initiated, "ride the wave" if the move is in your favor. If the move is contrary to your position, consider a hasty exit if the stock that you are trading is part of the S&P 500 Index. Remember, however, that futures and program trading are no more than an indicator for DayTraders. They are by no means the Holy Grail. Depending upon the weight of the other factors that you are considering, the movement of the futures index and program trading may or may not be significant in your evaluation of a trade.

10 Ticks

Second to the S&P Futures, the best forecasting tool that I have ever seen is the "Tick Indicator." It is a very simple Base Zero indicator that is derived by subtracting the number of downticking stocks from the number of upticking stocks.

The Ticks are a front running indicator for the S&P Futures and a great indicator for the general trend of the larger capitalization stocks, especially those of the Dow Industrial Average. When the Ticks are positive or negative 1,000 or more, a reversal (change in market direction) is in order. The only time that this does not hold true is when the market is surging or tanking, in which case prolonged periods of plus or minus 1,000 on the Ticks exists.

I have found that the one-minute bar chart is the best way to read the Ticks. The Ticks will trend, for the most part. However, when program trading or a strong shift in market sentiment takes place, the Ticks will spike 200-300 points or more in less than a minute. This is the best indication that program trading has been initiated. Additionally, it is a high probability indication of a reversal if the Ticks retrace more than 200 points in less than a minute, and an extremely high probability indication of a reversal if the Ticks retrace more than 300 points in the same amount of time. However, if the Ticks reverse sharply in the two minutes following the spike, disregard the indicator, and be very careful if you have entered a position based primarily on the Tick spike.

At the open, the Ticks are an excellent indicator of a reversal. On more days than not, the market will start out strong and then settle in. By paying close attention to the Ticks, it is possible to anticipate the settling of the market and position yourself to profit from this phenomenon a few days per week. There is, however, one caveat to this strategy. If there is news behind a strong trending market, don't use this strategy. If news is the cause of a surging or tanking market, any movement in the Ticks might be a temporary stall or retracement, with a continuation of trend in the wings.

There is a Tick Indicator for both the NYSE and Nasdaq markets. The NYSE Tick Indicator is the only one that I have ever used. Because of the nature of Nasdaq's dealer market, there is a lot of uptick and downtick volatility that makes the Nasdaq Ticks far less reliable than the specialist system (which trends more smoothly and is less volatile).

Scalping the Ticks...

The only time that I ever base trades solely on Tick spikes is with large-cap Dow stocks. In fact, this is one of my favorite scalping plays. When the Ticks spike, it is very easy to take an eighth or a quarter out of the likes of GE, DD, or JPM.

A variation of the Ticks is the Arms Index, which is most commonly known as TRIN. TRIN is a market indicator that shows the relationship between the number of stocks increasing or decreasing in price (advancing/declining issues) and the volume associated with stocks increasing or decreasing in price (advancing/declining volume). The index shows whether volume is flowing into advancing or declining stocks. If more volume is associated with advancing stocks than declining stocks, the TRIN will be less than 1.0. If more volume is associated with declining stocks, the index will be greater than 1.0. The formula for TRIN is:

$$\frac{\left(\dfrac{\text{Advancing Issues}}{\text{Declining Issues}}\right)}{\left(\dfrac{\text{Advancing Volume}}{\text{Declining Volume}}\right)}$$

Used in conjunction with the Ticks, TRIN can be a valuable confirming indicator. However, the disadvantage of the TRIN indicator is that it is volume weighted, which essentially smoothes out the data. The net result of this smoothing of data is that it is less reactive than the Ticks, and as a result it is not as great a front-running indicator.

By using the S&P Futures, Ticks, and TRIN to anticipate market movement, you will be better able to predict the movements of the stocks you are trading. However, if you are going to use these indicators to assist you in your entry and exit strategies, it is crucial that you know whether the stock you are considering is "with," "against," or "neutral" to the trend of the overall market. If you do not know the correlation, these indicators can give contrary and or misleading signals. (The topic of correlation is explained in "The Correlation Coefficients", Chapter 14 of this book.) [2]

11 Technicals

The question of the effectiveness of technical analysis is probably as old as securities trading itself. Some traders swear by it, while others consider it to be complete nonsense. The purpose of this chapter is not to teach technical analysis. Rather, it is to shed some light on this controversial question and give the reader a clear understanding of the benefits and limitations of incorporating technical analysis into trading strategies.

The most basic technical tool is the price/time chart, which graphically displays security price movement over time. For some, being able to "see" a picture of price movement is easier to interpolate than analyzing a series of numbers. To this end, there is no disagreement in terms of utility gained from this method of representation. However, when the issue of how to analyze this data enters the picture, the controversy begins.

Most of the time the vast majority of technical indicators are about as useful as flipping a coin. However, depending upon the security being analyzed, the sector that the security falls into, and the nature of the overall market, some technicals can be accurate predictors of price movement. Obviously there is no technical indicator that will perfectly predict future price movements. If there were one, the inventor would certainly never share it with anyone. Therefore, when considering the effectiveness of a particular technical indicator, it is helpful to think in terms of "probability of success." Any technical indicator exhibiting a probability of success greater than 50 percent is a useful tool (at least more so than your average coin).

For instance, when a stock is in a sideways pattern and trading within a tight range, the Bollinger Band can be a high probability indicator. Unfortunately, when a stock is in an upside breakout pattern, the upper arm of the Bollinger Band will be pressed against the graph of the stock itself, offering no effective prediction of price movement.

The question then arises: "How do I determine what technicals to use, and under what conditions?" The answer lies in the time frame being considered. There are no technical patterns that will effectively predict price movement indefinitely. For some securities, such as United States T-Bills, Notes, and Bonds, long-term trends that last from months to many years can be seen. For equities, patterns tend to be of a shorter-term nature. There are, of course, exceptions to the rule. The point is that securities display specific, predictable patterns that will last for varying periods of time. Therefore, because of the fluctuating nature of the market, technical indicators are effective only until the current pattern changes.

For example, intraday technicals are often inaccurate predictors of "microterm" price movements. The reason for this is that there are so many intraday crosscurrents of buying and selling pressure. Often, it is close to impossible to determine the degree to which intraday crosscurrents contribute to the "microterm" movement of stock prices.

When institutions such as Goldman Sachs, Merrill Lynch, Fidelity, and Berkshire Hathaway initiate large volume buy and sell programs in individual stocks, intraday price trends will reveal themselves in price/time charts. In some cases, more than one institution will initiate the same directional program in a given equity. When this happens, movements will be more dramatic and will usually be confirmed by an abnormal volume breakout. When institutions initiate opposing directional programs, whipsawing price patterns will reveal themselves, confirmed by abnormal volume patterns. If institutional buying and selling patterns were the only variable to be considered, intraday price movements would be more consistent and technical indicators could be used to more effectively predict intraday price movement. However, other variables strongly influence price movement on an intraday basis, making technical analysis ineffective in many cases.

One such variable is the institutional program trading of baskets of equities, which can cause rapid price swings. Because program trading is usually initiated at specific price levels, many firms often initiate program trades within seconds of one another. This type of computerized buying and selling of baskets of equities can overwhelm the aforementioned directional buying and selling of particular equities. In addition to institutional program trading, the introduction of individual DayTraders has created an environment of whipsawing price patterns.

Back in 1989, when the DayTrading industry began to reveal itself in the over the counter marketplace, there were very few DayTraders. Price movements were still dominated by the institutions, and DayTraders were often the "tail being wagged by the dog." Today, there are thousands, if not tens of thousands, of U.S. equity DayTraders controlling an estimated 15 to 25 percent of the average daily volume of the listed and over the counter market. Some equities, such as MSFT, AMZN, INTC, and YHOO, are largely influenced by the buying and selling patterns of DayTraders...who are now considered by many to be "the tail wagging the dog."

In addition to institutional buying and selling of specific equities, institutional program trading, and DayTrading, the retail investor also plays a large part in the overall behavior of the equity markets. Some investors self-direct their portfolios, while others pool their equity into mutual funds, index funds, and various other forms of "managed" investment mediums. The net flow of money into and out of managed funds will influence the direction of the overall market over time. During the past decade, there has been a net inflow of capital into the U.S. equity markets because of the strength of the U.S. economy and other variables. This has created buying pressure for stocks that have consistently outstripped supply, thus causing prices to trend upward over the long term.

In the short term, however, rotational repositioning of capital from one stock or sector to another creates a pattern of fluctuating prices. For example, INTC, which has been gaining in price consistently over the past four years, has experienced intermediate periods of price decline. Behind these movements (or retracements) is the combination of institutional, retail, and DayTrader buying and selling.

Once you understand the relative effectiveness of technical indicators over different time frames, the next step is to determine which technical indicator(s) provide predictive properties. The easiest way to accomplish this goal is to "eyeball" different technical indicators against the equity that you are analyzing. What I am describing here is a simple form of back testing. By varying the time frame being analyzed with each of the technical tools in your arsenal, patterns will reveal themselves.

Once a pattern is revealed, the next step is to confirm the pattern. With all technical indicators, volume is one of the best confirmations. With any sharp price movement, if volume does not increase, it is usually an indication of a "weak" breakout, and one that should be approached with caution. For sideways trends, any variance in the average daily volume over a period of days can often be a revealing indication of an upcoming change in pattern. Keep in mind that even volume (as a confirming indicator of price movement) is never 100 percent accurate.

In addition to volume, other technical analysis tools can be used as confirming indicators as well. When using other technical indicators in this role, I have found it most beneficial to use what I call "Planetary Alignment." Simply put, some "planets" are larger than others, thus carrying more weight or "gravitational pull." Some planets are very small, and have very little gravitational pull. Depending upon the security being analyzed, different planets will have different sizes and weights, which are continuously changing over time. With careful analysis, it is possible to uncover windows of opportunity in which a number of planets align. With no planets in alignment, one should be wary of entering into a trade based on a single indicator. The greater the number of planets that are in alignment, the greater the probability of success that the trader can expect to realize.

The Elephant Effect...

This information is found in the buying and selling patterns of large institutions. When Warren Buffet, George Soros, or the Fidelity Magellan Fund implements a buy or sell strategy, the price of that particular issue will begin to move. In a way, it is a self-fulfilling prophecy. If George Soros wants to accumulate five percent of a company, he will do so as quietly as possible. He does this quietly because if he were to announce on CNBC that he was about to begin accumulating a particular stock, market participants would invariably pounce on the stock, driving up the price. George would then have to pay a higher average price for the stock, and thus reduce his overall profit potential for this particular trade. Therefore, he will covertly accumulate the stock over a period of time, being careful not to raise the average daily trading volume to a level that would alert other market participants. Regardless of how careful he is, his action alone will create a supply/demand imbalance and push the price of the stock higher (unless, of course, another equally large market participant is selling an equal amount of the stock over the same time period).

One might think that following the buy and sell patterns of a George Soros would be quite simple...just watch what his fund is doing. This is easier said than done. The Georges of the world are very savvy, and have a huge arsenal of tricks and strategies to elude the herd of bloodhounds sniffing out their every move. Therefore, the only way the average investor can effectively ferret out the buying and selling patterns of the "elephants" (like Warren and George) is to watch the volume and price patterns of different stocks. (There are other ways to "see" these patterns — such as watching the volatility and outstanding interest in the underlying options — but they are beyond the scope of this book.)

The easiest way to capitalize on "The Elephant Strategy" is to watch the chart and the average daily trading volume. The elephant hides there! Any bullish or bearish trend, confirmed by increased volume, is often the footprint of the elephant. When volume subsides and the trend continues, it is a sign that the elephant has stopped moving, and it is time to cash out. One caveat is what sometimes appears to be an elephant is really a large herd of lost sheep chasing after a tasty pasture, or running from what they think is a hungry wolf.

The most difficult aspect of using technical indicators is that technicals are historical, and what the trader is attempting to do is predict the future. History does repeat itself, and historical patterns do rematerialize over time. The goal of technical analysis is to find a trend in progress and capitalize on it before the trend dissipates. Once a pattern has been identified and confirmed by Planetary Alignment, it is time to act.

When capitalizing on intermediate technical movements on an intraday basis, the strategy of buying, selling, short selling, and standing on the sideline requires timing. Even the strongest trends and patterns whipsaw. Because of this, you could be 100 percent correct in your intermediate technical analysis and still lose money on an intraday trade. Timing is clearly the key to DayTrading.

In terms of intraday trading of intermediate-term technical trends, four actions can occur. There can be a continuation, retracement, stall ("timeout"), or a reversal (contrary move that breaks the pattern). By analyzing the intraday movements in a particular equity over a period of days or weeks, you can get a "feel" for the intraday movements within an intermediate pattern. Once you have a feel for the "micro" movements in a stock, you can effectively time yourself into and out of trades on that particular stock. There is no real magic to timing. It is merely a function of paying close attention to the "micro" movements in a stock and reacting accordingly. With enough patience, time, and effort, anyone can pick up on the idiosyncrasies that every stock exhibits.

Depending upon which market or exchange a security is listed on, intraday "micro" movements in a stock will vary. Securities listed on the Nasdaq over the counter market are generally more volatile than securities listed on the New York Stock Exchange (NYSE)...and are subject to considerable intraday whipsawing within intermediate patterns.

The reason for the difference in volatility lies in the way securities are traded on the various exchanges. Nasdaq over the counter securities are traded in a market maker (or "dealer") market. Depending upon the number of market makers trading individual securities, the volatility will differ. The more market makers in a stock, the higher the potential for disagreement. Thus, there will be more whipsawing of price. Securities listed on the NYSE are traded in a specialist (or auction) market. Because the specialist's job is to "maintain a fair and orderly market" (as defined by the NYSE), he or she "smoothes out" the price of the stock by more efficiently matching up buyers and sellers and providing personal liquidity in the stock at various price levels. Although there are exceptions to the rule, the aforementioned has held true over the past decade or so on a top down (or "overall") level.

One final aspect of technical analysis to consider is the "self-fulfilling prophecy effect." Because technical analysis is so widely used by market participants, there is a "herd" of traders looking for the same patterns. A perfect example is a sideways price movement that exhibits a concave volume matrix. The volume traded in the stock subsides when the sideways price pattern begins, continues to decline during the sideways price movement, and then picks up. When the volume picks up, technicians (traders who base trading strategies on technical analysis of chart patterns) see a widely known pattern called a "saucer formation." Typically, the price chart will show a slight upward or downward movement concurrent with the rise in average daily trading volume. When the saucer forms, technicians view the upward or downward price bias as the beginning of a breakout. While there is some truth to the origin of this technical tool, the saucer formation has been further compounded by the fact that so many people are aware of this pattern and position themselves accordingly. This in turn becomes a self-fulfilling prophecy.

By reading a number of different books on technical analysis, you will quickly learn what the popular patterns are. Just because the patterns are popular, however, does not mean that a self-fulfilling prophecy will actually take place. Stronger crosscurrents exist in the marketplace that can overwhelm this variable, so beware.   On the other hand, if a popular technical pattern presents itself, and is in alignment with the other planets, the probability of self-fulfillment is quite high. Over time you will get a feel for what stocks "like" the various technical tools.   You will also get a feel for what patterns exhibit a high probability of self-fulfillment in different stocks.   As usual, careful study, patience, and diligence will pay off for those who are willing to pay attention for extended periods of time.

12 FACT VS. OPINION: WHAT MOVES THE MARKETS

To understand the equity market, one needs to understand its makeup, and what drives it. The "market" is the sum total of all participants in the "universe" that you define. The "universe" can be defined as the Dow Industrial Average, the S&P 500 Index, the Russell 2000 Index, the Biotech sector, the Banking sector, or even a particular stock. If the universe is the Dow Industrial Average, then the market is every trader, investor, specialist, fund manager, index fund, or hedge fund that is participating (or consciously choosing to not participate) in each and every stock in the Dow. If the universe is a particular stock, then the market consists of those who are participating (or choosing to not participate) in that particular issue.

Given a particular market, let's say the market for INTC, there are market makers, investors, traders, and fund managers evaluating and making buy and sell decisions in that stock. (Remember that doing nothing is still a decision - it is a decision to not act.) Each decision that is made by each individual market participant will vary in terms of timing, strategy, duration, risk tolerance, etc. Each individual market participant, depending upon the decision that he or she makes, will cause one of three things to happen: added demand for the stock, added supply of the stock, or the addition of neither demand nor supply.

The sum total of all the supply, demand, timing strategies, duration, risk tolerance, etc., is represented in the price/time graph of the stock. Another way to describe what the chart represents is to say that the chart is a sentiment indicator of all market participants.

Sentiment is, by definition, opinion. It is not a fact, but rather what people think. Sentiment is based on all of the information or input used to make the decision to buy, sell, or do nothing at all. A widely held belief is that all available public information is represented in the price of a stock, and thus, the value of the stock is representative of the interpreted meaning and value of all available public information.

As new pieces of information are made public, all market participants must digest that information and re-evaluate their sentiment in the stock. The newly re-evaluated sentiments are then represented in the market, based on the decisions that each participant makes. Of course, opinions vary. Regardless, the sum total of all opinions will be represented in the price of the stock. It is for this reason that when a new piece of heavily weighted information is released to the public, price movements occur. If the information affects a broad category of stocks, then price movements will be more widespread.

Once all market participants have had the opportunity to evaluate the new information, the market will settle at a new price. Because individuals react to information at varying rates and with varying degrees of magnitude, it will be some time before price movements take full effect. In the absence of new information, volatility will typically decline and will not resume until new information is added to the mix.

There are degrees in which information is available. On one end of the scale is nonpublic information, which is illegal to base trading decisions on. On the other end of the spectrum is news that blankets the planet via the global media machine. Within this spectrum lies information that is readily available to anyone who wants it, such as annual reports, 10Ks, and 10Qs. There is also information, such as real-time news, that is only available to those who are willing to pay for it. It is because of this range of "public-ness" of information that it takes different periods of time for market participants to react to and digest news.

When a new piece of information becomes public, it is important to formulate an opinion as to the weight and meaning of that news. It is also important to take into consideration how the sum total of all market participants will interpret this information. Even if you feel very strongly that a piece of information is very bullish for INTC, the rest of the market may not see things the same way that you do. Consider who the other participants are. Evaluate how long it will take for the majority of market participants to get and interpret the news. Anticipate what the market will do, rather than what YOU think is the right thing to do. You may find that your opinion is in sync with the market, and you may find that it is not.

If you are always dead wrong about how a piece of information will affect the price of a stock, this alone is a very powerful indicator. If you think one way, and you feel that the market is going to "think" the other way, go with the market. As you know, "If you can't beat 'em, join 'em."

Note, however, that going against what you feel is a very difficult strategy to implement. I have a knack for picking the wrong direction in Eli Lilly (LLY). Unfortunately, each time I have tried to make a decision and then go the other way, I have lost. It is hard to form an opinion about something and then do the opposite. My mind seems to be one step ahead of me on this one, and tricks me into thinking the opposite of what I usually think, so that I still end up doing what I usually do. I guess I could just do the opposite of the opposite of what I was thinking I should do, but that probably wouldn't work either. For those of you who are able to make this work, please give me a call. I need some coaching.

13 HOMEWORK

As my second grade teacher always told me, "If you don't do your homework, you will never learn." The same holds true for DayTraders. "If you don't do your homework, you will never learn." Eventually you may fail as a DayTrader and be forced to change "majors." Required reading for this course begins with annual reports, 10Qs, and 10Ks, which you can order directly from companies. Ask your broker if he or she has additional reports on the stocks that you are researching. Use search engines on the web to gather information. Visit company web sites. Most (if not all) public companies have web sites. These sites can be the source of more information than you will ever want to know.

Remember, just because information is published does not mean it is necessarily true or unbiased. Take all information with a grain of salt, and seek as much information from as many sources as possible. Take the sum total of your research and develop your own opinion. This is how the professional analysts do their research.

By following the methods of the professionals, you may be able to develop the same conclusions that they do and position yourself to capitalize on impactful analysts' recommendations before they make them public. In addition to putting yourself in a position to anticipate and capitalize on analysts' recommendations, you will also be learning what the big players already know. By doing this (in conjunction with watching the charts and their underlying volume) you will be able to better predict the timing, duration, and size of price movements.

In addition to knowing what the analysts and the big players already know, a keen understanding of a particular stock will enable you, the trader, to better interpret all types of news as it is made public. You will be better prepared to size up the impact that different news releases will have, and you will enhance your ability to weigh related news stories.

At first you may get frustrated with the amount of time that you devote to research, and you may not see immediate results in terms of improved trading and overall profitability. Over time, your research will accumulate in your mind, and what you will inevitably find is that your understanding of stocks (and the market in general) will increase.

It takes years, not weeks or months, to truly get a feel for how the stock market acts, reacts, and does not react to different scenarios, time frames, and circumstances. Trading for a living is not easy, and it requires considerable time and effort to be truly successful. A part-time effort will either yield a part-time salary or a net loss of capital. My experience with traders that do not take their chosen profession seriously is that they end up changing professions. Diligent, disciplined, dedicated traders consistently beat the S&P average, and are very profitable and happy with their chosen profession.

Over time, your research will pay off in spades (and dollars). Try not to get frustrated. If you do, try taking it out on an annual report or a good book on trading strategies. Focus your energy on learning from your mistakes, and learning from those who are more knowledgeable. Give yourself the luxury of time to learn how to trade successfully. Don't get greedy or impatient. If you don't like the trading day today and you don't have a good feel for what the market is going to do, don't trade. Sometimes the best trade is no trade at all. Use "off" days to study and learn from what the market has to say to you. It is constantly telling a story. If you listen, rather than fight the market and try to 'eek out lucky gains, you will be happily paying more money to the government in taxes at the end of the year. If you fight the market, the IRS will be offering you a tax loss carry forward. The choice is yours.

Time and time again, I hear traders say that they cannot take time off from the market because trading is how they make a living. If you have been trading for a while, I am sure there were a few periods that you wish you had taken off. Trading does not translate into income every day. You will always have losing days. Knowing, understanding, and accepting that there are certain market conditions that you do not yet understand is the key to limiting your losses during these periods. If you choose to sit on the sideline during a market phenomenon that you don't understand, I guarantee that you will not lose any money. If you sit on the sideline and study the market, as opposed to taking a vacation in the south of France, you may be able to make money in the market the next time the same environment presents itself. Remember, history repeats itself over and over again. What the market did today, yesterday, or 100 years ago, the market will do again at some point in the future.

When you listen to others and base your trading strategies on their research and opinions, you do not know all that there is to know. You do not know all of the variables and caveats that they are considering, and you are somewhat blind to various potential outcomes (which are based upon continuously unfolding events). If you don't do your own homework, and you make trading decisions based solely on what someone else tells you, then you will not be as well informed. If you are taking advice from a great trader, you will most likely make money. However, you probably won't make nearly as much as the person that you are taking advice from!

History repeats itself...

There are some days that I have seen before. I just "know" what is going to happen and when it is going to happen. Here is an example to clarify my point.

On a Friday in the middle of August 1997, a trading day that I had seen many times before came to be. The analysis that I was performing at that time gave strong indications that such a day was coming. I spent the week before this day not trading, but researching the market. That particular Friday was smack in the middle of "The Dog Days of Summer" and preceded a key Federal Reserve meeting the following Tuesday. I knew that no one would want to worry about the sizeable positions that they were holding just before the Fed met. I knew this because I had seen it before.

The weekend before this momentous date, I stayed home in my upper east-side apartment in Manhattan and

---

researched the market. I read the most recent issue of Barron's three times and found the Barron's issues from July of 1996 preceding and following the correction that year. (I never throw out my Barron's and have a severe fire hazard sitting under my bed.) I surfed the web and used the Bloomberg machine at my friend's office. I read the Wall Street Journal and Investors Business Daily from the previous two weeks, cover to cover.

My plan for this day was to make more money in one day than I had made all year. During the week, I stopped researching, and started listening to the market. I watched objectively and noted what I saw. Monday was unclear, Tuesday was clearer, Wednesday was exciting. At this point, all of the planets were coming into alignment for the big day. ("Planetary Alignment" was explained in detail in "Technicals," Chapter 11 of this book.) The market was chopping along, showing increased trading volume in a sideways, volatile pattern …just what I was looking for. The key variable, the weather, even cooperated. Two days before this particular Friday, I saw the five-day forecast. There was not a cloud in the sky from New York to California. Clear, sunny skies were forecast for the entire weekend with temperatures in the mid 80s. I knew that the majority of Wall Street would either be in the Hamptons or on the Jersey Shore with friends and family. Without a beautiful weekend, I feared Wall Streeters would stay home that weekend and not liquidate their holdings as readily as they would if they were looking forward to a worry-free, relaxing weekend on the ocean.

Thursday was further confirmation. The trading volume was not abnormal, but the sideways pattern continued, and volatility increased in the issues I was targeting.

I could barely sleep on Thursday night and was at the Bloomberg machine at 4:30 a.m. the next morning. I figured that the day would be volatile and biased to the downside, with two or three strong rallies. When the market opened, I waited and did nothing. When the Ticks and the futures started to cave, I started to implement my plan. I had on my "hit list" the big issues: JP Morgan, GE, DuPont, Exxon, and IBM. I had narrowed this list down to five from about 20 over the course of the week (based on specific criteria that I was looking for).

I offered all of these stocks short, setting myself up to exceed my buying power. I anticipated that because these stocks were starting to downtick when I offered them short, I would be able to max out my capital and cancel the rest of the orders. My strategy worked surprisingly well, and I was able to stay within my buying power. I stayed short until the Ticks and the futures changed direction, and then waited for two upticks in a row in the stocks that I was short. When this happened, I bought back the shares, waited for another uptick as confirmation of the reversal, and went long the issues that were lagging the average. I did this all day long. By three o'clock I had done about 15 trades. I had losing positions on two trades, and averaged ½ point profit on the rest.

This was the first of a two-part strategy. I didn't know whether or not the market would rally before caving in during the last 20 minutes of trading, so I sat patiently on the sideline after 3:00 p.m. The market did rally, and sharply. I could have made quite a bit of money, had I gone long at this point, but my strategy was to get short…and I didn't think the rally would be a sustained one. (I was actually surprised how strong it was.) The market, which was in negative territory all day long, almost went positive. Surprised as I was, I "knew" it would not go into positive territory and I anticipated that within 30 points of positive, the final sell-off would begin. At - 40 on the day, with the market still rallying, I started offering GE short, because it looked overextended and had started to go sideways on considerable volume.

As soon as I had the desired short position in GE, I saw DuPont level off and start to spike in volume so I offered it short. The Ticks started to fade at that point and then spiked downward about 300 points within a minute. This was a clear indication that sell programs had been initiated.

No sooner did I get short all of the shares of DuPont that I had offered, a large sell imbalance came across the Bloomberg on DuPont. This sell imbalance was followed by sell imbalances in about half of the Dow Industrial Average stocks. The Ticks continued to tank, followed by the futures. The Ticks bottomed out in the negative 1400 range and never looked up. The market dropped nearly 250 points in the last 20 minutes of trading that day: August 15, 1997.

I logged off of my computer at the end of the day with more than a 50 percent gain in my capital. (I was working for a hedge fund at the time, and had quite a bit of leverage on my personal capital.) The total return for the day based on the total capital that I had utilized was more than 10 percent. I left for the Hamptons that afternoon a very happy and considerably richer man.

Had I gone to the Hamptons like all of my friends the previous weekend, and traded like all of my colleagues during the week, I too might have been a net loser of capital that day (as was the case with many of my colleagues, who were still long when the market caved in). You are probably thinking that I was quite selfish not to share my research. That was not the case. I told my friends what I thought, but they chose not to listen. I respect the fact that they didn't listen. I could have been wrong. The market could have shot up 250 points that day, and I would have been a big loser.

Ultimately, traders must make their own trading decisions. The other traders' decisions that day were based on their own homework and their own interpretation of available information. Had the other traders done the same research that I had done, they may have come to the same conclusion that I had. Then again, they may not have. That is the nature of the beasts that we call "bulls" and "bears."

The moral of this story is not that I am the greatest trader in the world. I'm not. The moral is:

"DO YOUR HOMEWORK,
AND YOU WILL BE REWARDED."

This is not to say that you should never take advice from others. In fact, I suggest that you listen to as many people as possible, watch them, learn from their strategies, and profit from trading opportunities that you too are knowledgeable about. If your friend always trades ANET, and he calls you on the phone and demands that you buy it now, be wary. Perhaps the best course of action is to pass on this particular trade and do some research on the company, its sector, and the general trends, and news surrounding both that stock and the sector. The next time your friend calls and demands that you buy the stock, you will be prepared to evaluate the potential of the trade and make an educated decision.

In terms of taking advice from others, remember, it is not just your friends giving advice. All magazines, books, newspapers, analysts, editors, broker dealers, newsletters, and mutual funds are giving biased advice. Even if the author is being 100 percent objective, he or she is using biased research material to formulate his or her article. Be wary (not paranoid, but wary) of everything you see, hear, or read. The only information that is not biased is mine.

Just kidding. The best way to formulate a biased, yet knowledgeable, opinion of your own is to tap into as many sources of information as possible and form your own conclusion. My advice is not to TRY to formulate an opinion. Quite the contrary, my advice is to try to remain as objective as humanly possible. The opinion will come naturally — when you are sitting at your computer contemplating whether or not to enter a trade. Your opinion will become apparent in the decision you make to buy, sell, sell short, or do nothing at all. In trading, there is no easier way to clarify your opinion than to trade (or not trade) based on your research. Don't waste time and energy trying to form an opinion. Focus your efforts on research.

What I have learned about researching the stock market is that I cannot remember all of the numbers and names that I have read, seen, and heard. However, a funny thing goes on upstairs. Although I cannot actively recall these facts and figures, they are there and are regurgitated as gut instinct. I could never quantify all of the variables that went into my decision to trade the way that I did on August 15, 1997. What alerted me to the opportunity was part experience, part research, and part intuition. What I do know is that my intuition is not luck. My intuition is the result of nearly a decade of diligent research and time consuming study of the financial markets.

I have a feel for the financial markets that I will never lose (unless I take a good whack on the head). I am carefully risky, and I am someone who does not appreciate gambling. I consider my past successes and failures (I prefer to call them learning experiences) to be the fruit of my labor. I do not believe that some people "got it," and some people "don't." My belief is that anyone that has discipline, patience, desire, the right attitude, and a reasonable IQ can be a successful trader. The key element in the short term is patience. Give yourself the luxury of time to learn and grow as a trader. If you get too aggressive at the outset, you may find very quickly that you no longer have enough capital to trade and you will have to look for a day job. This will only further delay you from your goal of being a successful, professional trader.

14 CORRELATION COEFFICIENTS

In today's financial markets, a relationship or correlation exists between all securities. Sometimes there is a positive correlation, sometimes there is a negative correlation, and sometimes there is no correlation whatsoever. What I am describing is often referred to as a correlation coefficient.

A correlation coefficient is described by a range which spans from negative one to positive one (-1, 1). Securities that are positively correlated will move in tandem with one another, and stocks that are negatively correlated will move opposite one another.

For example, let's assume that DELL and CPQ have a positive correlation. If they are 100 percent positively correlated (+ 1), then a one point move in DELL would be followed by a one-point move in CPQ, or vice versa. If these two stocks are 50 percent positively correlated (+.5), then a one point move in DELL would be followed by a 1/2 point move in CPQ, or vice versa. If these two stocks have no correlation whatsoever (0), then a one point move in DELL would not cause CPQ to move at all.

When stocks are positively or negatively correlated, movement in one stock is followed by movement in other correlated stocks. The degree of correlation, positive or negative, will determine to what degree prices of correlated stocks move. Because different stocks have some degree of correlation to one another, it is easy to understand that different sectors (which are made up of groups of correlated stocks) are correlated to one another. Taking this concept one step further, it becomes clear why there is a correlation between different broad market averages, such as the Dow Industrials, the S&P 500 and the Russell 2000. One can also see why different global markets are correlated to one another (to varying degrees).

Regardless of whether you are considering a stock, sector, broad average, future, bond, commodity, or currency, all securities react to different types of information. As an example, let's use a war in the Middle East that may cause oil prices to rise. In the oil sector, Mobil, Texaco, and the other oil stocks will almost always increase in price over time. The reason for this is that oil companies have vast reserves of oil. The cost to drill, pump, and refine oil into a usable product is generally fixed. Therefore, higher oil prices fatten the bottom line of these companies in the short term, and thus drive up the prices of these stocks.

Higher oil prices also translate into higher fuel costs for the airline industry. Since all other costs associated with the operation of an airline company are relatively fixed, an increase in fuel costs will thin out the bottom line of American Airlines, Delta, and the other airline companies. The net result of this ripple effect is lower stock prices in the airline sector. One might argue that if the cost of jet fuel goes up, airlines could simply increase fare prices. (However, unlike oil consumption, airline travel is elastic, meaning that "consumption" of airline tickets will fluctuate with the price level of airline tickets.) Thus, when fare prices rise, the number of airline travelers decreases, and the net result is still decreased profits.

In this example, it is clear that a negative correlation exists between the Airline sector and the oil sector. Stepping outside of the world of equities, a war in the Middle East might also spark fears of inflation. Because oil is one of our nation's base commodities, a prolonged increase in oil prices will eventually seep into every corner of our economy. If the cost of base commodities increases, the long-term result will be higher prices, or inflation. When inflation rears its ugly head, the Federal Reserve will raise interest rates to cool off the economy. When interest rates rise, bond prices will fall. Ergo, it can be said that a prolonged increase in oil prices may spark a decrease in bond prices.

While oil prices typically react immediately to an outbreak of war in the Middle East, it may be minutes, hours, days, or weeks before oil and airline stocks exhibit a price reaction to this news. Similarly, the time frame in which oil stocks react to this news will vary from the time frame in which airline stocks will react. The magnitude and severity of the news will determine how quickly related securities exhibit price reactions. Therefore, a trader not only needs to know the correlation coefficient between different stocks, he/she also needs to know the time frame in which different securities will react.

To complicate matters even more, correlation coefficients are not constants, and they too will adjust over time. Some correlation coefficients will remain constant for years or even decades, while other correlation coefficients will adjust on a daily, weekly, and monthly basis. Typically, the correlation coefficient between individual securities will adjust on a weekly to monthly basis. Correlation coefficients between market sectors will typically adjust on a monthly to yearly basis. Commodities will tend to adjust on a much broader time frame, spanning from years to decades. Broad industry averages, such as the Dow Industrial Average and the Nasdaq Composite Index, tend to adjust anywhere from weeks to years.

Depending on the magnitude of the news and the variables that affect different securities, shifts in correlation coefficients can range from nonexistent to dramatic. The time frames during which these shifts occur can also vary dramatically. Consequently, constant research and careful study is needed to remain on top of shifting correlation coefficients that exist within financial markets.

Because stocks react to news over varying time frames, a forecasting effect exists. In other words, when a piece of news comes out that immediately affects the price of a particular stock, there is a time delay between the price movement of that stock and the stocks that are correlated to it. When a piece of news causes a dramatic spike in the price of a particular issue, I have found it is terribly difficult to determine whether that stock will continue or retrace the price movement. In my opinion, the chance of picking the intraday direction of a stock that is "already in play" is about equal to flipping a coin. To trade a stock in this situation is gambling, in my opinion, and I always pass on that trade.

However, given the fact that the price of a particular issue has spiked, and that all stocks are correlated to one degree or another (even a correlation of zero is a form of correlation), "secondary" price movements are not far away. (Using the "primary" price movement as an "alert," I focus my attention on "secondary" movements, and position my capital in anticipation of correlated price movement.)

Over time, patterns of correlation and timing will reveal themselves to those who are patient and diligent enough to seek them out. If you do not have a program that delivers correlation coefficients, you will need to map them manually. I recommend using a spreadsheet program to log and analyze your data. When a piece of news comes out on one stock, the place to capitalize is in strongly correlated securities and not the security that the news directly affected. By far, the safest correlation play is what I call "Spread Trading," which is the next topic of discussion.

15 SPREAD TRADING

When a trader places a trade, two types of risk exist: stock-specific and market risk. Stock-specific risk can only be reduced through careful timing. The skill of timing can be enhanced through careful research of the equity being traded and a thorough understanding of what causes price reactions in that particular issue. However, if the timing is not right, a trader can lose money in any stock, regardless of how much the stock might be worth 10 days or 10 years from now. Remember, we are talking about DayTrading here, not long-term investing.

Market risk (also known as systemic risk) is the risk that a conflicting move in the broader market will pull the stock that you are trading in the opposite direction of your trade. Systemic risk cannot be completely eliminated while still leaving the opportunity for profit. For example, if a trader were to go long a stock in one account, and then short the same stock in a second account, he/she would (net) neither be long nor short. This is what is referred to as delta neutral, flat, or fully hedged. Any price movement in the stock will have zero effect on the trader's capital balance. If the market were to crash, the trader would neither gain nor lose money. Unfortunately, with this arrangement there is no way for the trader to profit.

Another way to mitigate market risk is to implement an options or futures strategy, but that is beyond the scope of this book. In terms of DayTrading stocks, the best way to mitigate systemic risk (while still retaining the opportunity to profit) is to implement a "spread trade." Here is how it works:

Because stocks are positively and negatively correlated, it is possible to capitalize on a piece of news on both the long and short side. (For example, let's assume that there is a strong positive correlation between DELL and CPQ, and that a negative correlation existed between GTW and both DELL and CPQ.) Therefore, when a piece of bullish news comes out on DELL, it is possible to short GTW and go long CPQ at the same time. In this circumstance, GTW will lose ground, given the existing fears that CPQ and DELL are crushing GTW in the marketplace. Since DELL and CPQ are both strong companies, anything that is bullish for DELL is interpreted by market participants as bullish for CPQ, and vice versa. By going long and short two closely related stocks in the same sector, the risk associated with bearish news that affects the entire sector is mitigated. For example, the announcement of a flawed Intel chip would cause all computer manufacturers to decline in price. If a trader is long CPQ and short GTW, the impact of the Intel news will be "balanced" by the trader's position in the sector.

The advice that I will offer to traders who choose to implement this strategy is to consider offering short the negatively correlated stock before going long the positively correlated stock. Because of the uptick rule, it is much easier to go long than it is to get short. Keep in mind, however, that there is a varying time lag in terms of when correlated stocks react to news on another security. If you know that the long side of the spread trade is going to react quicker, then that is the "leg" to put on first.

Also, because you will be putting on two trades based on one piece of news, be cognizant of the amount of capital that you risk on the trade. The risk associated with a spread trade is that contrary news comes out on one of the stocks that you are spreading. In the event that this occurs, you will get "whacked" on both sides of the trade. This IS possible, but chances are that it will not happen. Therefore, if you make 20 spread trades, and one goes against you because of contrary news, you should still be well in the black on this strategy.

During the course of "non event" trading days, stocks will drift and sway with the industry sectors that they are a part of as well as with the market in general. In the absence of news, correlation coefficients are of little use in predicting price movements. During these periods of "quiet" market activity, you will have to look to other tools and strategies to ferret out trading opportunities.

DayTrading into the Millennium

16 TRADING THE SECTORS

The highest correlation between stocks exists between stocks in the same industry sector. Over time, there are always some sectors that are "hot," and some that are "not." Because there has been a net inflow of investor funds into the U.S. equity markets during the past decade of economic expansion, buying pressure has far outstripped selling pressure. Demand for stocks, paralleled by a strong economy and a plethora of profitable, growing companies (which is the primary cause for the demand in the first place), has caused stock prices to gain dramatically in value. The introduction of computers in every aspect of our economy has been the primary catalyst for this expansion (Bill Clinton might disagree with me here). Computers brought increased efficiency, reduced production costs, and economies of scale to almost every business in the nation. The average annual gains in the U.S. markets during the past five years far outstrips the average annual gains in the U.S. markets during the past 75 years.

Because of the continued influx of capital into managed funds, there is constant pressure on fund managers to invest in the market. Given the rules and guidelines of the different managed fund vehicles, many fund managers are required to stay invested in particular groups of stocks in quite specific percentages. Fund managers still have broad discretion over what particular issues to invest in. Nevertheless, they cannot stray too far from the design of the fund. For instance, a biotechnology fund manager cannot put all of the funds capital in the Banking sector, nor can he invest solely in GE. That same fund manager cannot put all of the fund's money in a money market fund and stay out of the market.

It is not to say that fund managers cannot hold large cash positions and time their entry and exit points in the market in specific issues that they have a propensity to trade. However, fund managers are graded against baselines (such as the S&P 500 Index) or against other fund managers. Given that most fund managers have the majority of the fund's capital invested in the market, and given the fact that the job of a fund manager is high paying, these types don't stray too far from the rest of the herd. If a fund manager is average, he still keeps his job. If a fund manager is above average, he still keeps his job. If a fund manager is below average or makes a catastrophic mistake, he does not keep his job. This mindset translates into a propensity for most fund managers to "stay the course" and not do something that will cost them the Porsche and house in the Hamptons.

Now that you understand the mindset of the fund manager, it is easier to comprehend why money, for the most part, stays in the market. It does, however, shift around from sector to sector. Funds that have very spe-cific guidelines are limited to the sectors and securities that they can be "rotated" through. Still, the majority of funds are designed to give managers broad latitude to shift and move the capital from sector to sector - and they do. Why do they do this?

Because everyone else does. This is half a joke, but half true. Sector rotation is as old as the sectors themselves. Depending upon the news du jour, different sectors are in play. Sometimes it is the Internet sector, sometimes the banking sector, the oil sector, transportation sector, hardware sector, or the biotech sector. The rotation is initiated by news events and is followed by the bandwagon effect of fund managers and other institutional investors following the herd. Finally, once the sector really heats up, the story hits the cover of Business Week, and the retail investors pile in. It is at this point that the big money looks elsewhere, and the cycle begins anew.

The telltale signs to look for in sector rotation are many fold. A series of positively biased news stories related to a sector will set off the herd. This is followed by upward trending stock prices, confirmed by increased volume. (Somewhat after the fact, investment banks and newsletters alike will come out with upgraded buy recommendations on stocks in that sector, which is typically followed by the media bandwagon.) Also after the fact, fund managers will begin to report their positions. This happens right around the time that the retail masses decide it is a smart investment.

Sector rotation is not an intraday event. It can last from weeks to months, and in rare cases, years. Therefore, there is quite a bit of time to recognize and capitalize on the sector rotation strategy. (The earlier one learns about it, the more one can profit...so it behooves the trader to keep a watchful eye out for what's "hot" and what's "not.")

To add this strategy to your arsenal, the best place to start is in your favorite sector. If you typically DayTrade in a sector that has relatively low volatility, like the Utility sector, for example, then you have problems. I would suggest picking one of the following sectors to begin with:

- Airline sector
- Banking sector
- Biotechnology sector
- Drug sector
- Hardware sector
- Internet sector
- Networking sector
- Oil sector
- Oil Peripherals sector
- Software sector

These are my favorites, and I have found that a handful of these sectors are always in play. You may find that another sector is more suitable to your background and training. If you spent 29 years working for International Paper, then perhaps the Paper sector would be the best place for you to start (as long as it is volatile). The bottom line is to choose the sector that you are most knowledgeable about. There are 30-plus "primary" sectors in the broad market. Some sectors are the combination of smaller sectors, which I call "peripheral sectors," of which there are a hundred or more.

Once you have chosen a sector, the next step is to choose a handful of stocks and begin researching them. Picking too many stocks to start with will spread you too thin. Picking too few stocks will not give you enough of a feel for the sector to accurately evaluate it from the top down. I would suggest starting with 5 or 10 stocks. Learn them intimately. Trade them whenever the opportunity arises. Research your trades in these stocks, and watch the patterns closely. Take notes on how different types of news affect the stocks' prices, and use these stocks as the basis for developing a feel for correlated stocks. Be diligent, and again, focus on just a handful of stocks to start.

Once you are comfortable with your first handful of stocks, grab another handful. The second handful will require more effort, because you are now doubling your universe of stocks. Not only will you be closely following and continuously researching the first handful of stocks, you will now have another group to study, learn, and observe.

A close friend of mine, Doug Weaver, described a method of grouping similar to the one that I use. He, however, uses a baseball team analogy of the four groups of stocks that he watches. He's got the starting lineup, the bullpen, the bench, and the minor leagues.

In the same way that the manager of a baseball team concentrates on his starting lineup and bullpen more than the "pine riders," I concentrate on my core group more than I do the secondary or tertiary group. "Minor leaguers" from the fourth group have their stats reviewed from time to time but are rarely invited to play.

As explained in the "Correlation Coefficients" chapter, there is a time delay in price action between even the most highly correlated stocks. (For example, knowing that there is bullish pressure in the entire sector, you can use the larger stocks in the sector in the same way that you use the Ticks or the S&P Futures as a forward-looking indicator.) There are always a handful of primary stocks that drive a sector. Using the correlations between these stocks (and knowing the time lags between the stocks in the sector) it is possible to trade a sector on the long and short side, day in and day out.

When there is significant buying pressure in a sector, it is time to buy the dips. Before buying the dips, however, be sure to look to the broader market and the most closely related sectors. You don't want to fade (go against) the broad market in most cases. When the broad market moves sharply, and the sector that you are trading follows suit, watch to see which stocks in the sector are fading the trend (or not following it to the degree in which the rest of the stocks in the sector are reacting to the movement).

Stocks that fade a bullish (bearish) trend will fall (rise) the fastest when the trend reverses. This is not written in stone but is written in very hard wood. Strong surges in sectors and broad market indices are great forecasting tools. Watch very closely when this happens, and you will see strength and weakness in the market. In the August 15, 1997 story that I described in the "Homework" chapter, this is what I was looking for. On the days before August 15 when I was not trading, I was looking for stocks that caved with the Dow. My strategy was confirmed all week long. Every time the Dow shook, either to the upside or the downside in a rapid swing, I watched and then whittled down my group of possible stocks. In other words, I benched the weak players and sent the weakest players down to the minors.

In my opinion, if you learn how to play the sectors,

you will be a successful trader. For me, this is by far the most profitable of all of my trading strategies. In the beginning, I was overwhelmed by the sheer number of stocks and the amount of information available on all of these stocks. Focusing on the Sector Rotation strategy was the turning point for me. It helped me to learn correlation coefficients, and it gave me direction in my research. It helped me focus on what was "hot" and forget about what was "not." Over the course of a few weeks, I went from being a marginally unprofitable trader to a reasonably successful trader.

I am admittedly not the world's best trader and have a lifetime to improve my strategies and refine my techniques. I review technical studies on a regular basis. I read books on the markets, not just about stocks, but futures, commodities, and foreign markets. For me it is not work. I have a passion for the markets. For me, reading about the markets is much better than any trashy supermarket romance novel. (I have quite a few friends that read the supermarket trash and I still love them. Oh well, to each their own.) Anyhow, my point is that if you have the luxury of time to learn about other financial markets, your understanding of sector rotation will be much more enhanced.

17 SOUP DU JOUR

From the beginning of time there have always been a few primary issues facing inhabitants of the world. Millions of years ago, how to walk on land was the issue. Later, the dinosaurs were more concerned with how to stay warm. Many years later, the making of fire was the topic of the day amongst cavemen. In more recent times, world wars, regional conflicts, terrorism, communism, disease, and infrastructure have spanned the headlines.

During the past few decades, the primary concern of participants in the equities market was inflation. All eyes were focused on Alan Greenspan and the economic indicators that he used to gauge inflation. Analysts across the globe would give estimates of these indicators and, as a collective group, traders would price these expectations into the market.

The topic of inflation has dominated the financial markets, ranging from currencies to bonds, futures, equities, and commodities. I can remember when a 5.2 percent inflation rate shocked the financial markets in the United States. In the late 1997 market, a sub 5.0 percent inflation rate was of little concern to anyone. The introduction of powerful computers has enabled companies to realize economies of scale created through mergers and acquisitions. Because of this shift, in conjunction with sophisticated modeling techniques the Federal Reserve now uses to gauge and control inflation, today's economy appears to be capable of warding off inflation. Some swear that the days of inflation are over. (Others believe that we can better manage inflation, but that it does and always will exist.) I believe the latter sentiment to be the most realistic.

With inflationary fears on the back burner during this period, there existed a need for a new soup du jour. Earnings season comes around four times a year and always takes center stage in today's equity market. However, earnings seasons pass. Something big was needed for market participants to sink their teeth into. Inflation was such a juicy issue that it would certainly be hard to top. It took some time, but sure enough, the analysts and the media were able to spin together a concoction that would not only rattle the foundation of the U.S. financial markets, but financial markets around the world.

What could possibly be so powerful and so world encompassing? How about the Asian Flu of 1997?! Indeed, the flu quickly found its way into the trade winds and jet streams and encompassed the world with lightning speed. Fear and panic set in, and before anyone could utter a word of rational dissent, the financial markets of the planet sharply corrected in a Halloween sell-off comparable to Black Monday (which, strangely enough, occurred almost exactly 10 years earlier).

There will always be a soup du jour that will act as the basis upon which to interpret all new information. When the soup du jour changes, a dramatic shift occurs.

It is critically important to factor these "shifts" into your trading equation. So important is it that I have devoted the next chapter to the further definition and explanation of these shifts.

DayTrading into the Millennium

18 PARADIGM SHIFTS

The term "Paradigm Shift" was explained to me a number of years back by my father, who is a widely known industrial engineer. He travels the nation as a consultant and teacher of The Theory of Constraint Management. He has consulted for a wide range of businesses, such as Caterpillar, Rockwell, National Semiconductor, and Sweetheart Cup. In his role, he reveals to the various people and companies he speaks to a different way of looking at their business. In essence, he attempts (through education and understanding) to shift the way his clients "see" their companies and the decisions they make. At some point in the process (if all goes well), clients "see the light," and the "world" of thoughts, ideas, concepts and truths that these clients "live in" makes an abrupt "shift."

What I am describing here is a paradigm shift. It is caused by a reaction to new information being introduced into an environment. When this happens, the effect (depending upon the magnitude of the new information) can be tremulous and dramatic. In each of our lives we experience paradigm shifts that, for lack of more eloquent terminology, "rock our world." Whether it is a death in the family, a divorce, or a winning lottery ticket, the effect of introducing such new information has a powerful, paradigm-shifting effect. Our previous vision of the future evaporates before our eyes. In most cases, it takes some time for the dust to settle. When it does, a new vision of the future appears, and the paradigm shift is complete.

This tremulous transition is similar to seeing your exit on the freeway a little late and veering off the highway at 60 miles per hour in an evasive maneuver. The tires may squeal and the person that you cut off may lean on the horn (and probably give you the finger). You may be able to navigate the sharp curve of the exit ramp and come to a stop with no damage to you or your car. However, you may hit the guardrail and put a big dent in your fender — which can be fixed. The worst case would be that you drive off the road, flip your car into a ravine, and die. In any event, there will always be an outcome, ranging from nothing noticeable to catastrophic. Assuming that you live to tell the tale, the shift in perception will reshape your future to varying degrees.

In the equities market, paradigm shifts occur constantly. Sometimes a paradigm shift occurs in a particular stock or sector, and sometimes it affects the entire market. Again, it is the type and the degree of magnitude of news that will be the "Richter Scale" and catalyst for the resulting effect.

Paradigm shifts are not always negative. In fact, many paradigm shifts are extremely positive, such as a winning lottery ticket, getting a better job offer, or becoming pregnant (debatable). When a paradigm shift occurs in the financial markets, the universe of participants will interpret the news over varying periods of time and adjust their individual ways of thinking to incorporate the new information. On a macro or "global" level, the net sum of these individual paradigm shifts will translate into an overall shift in perception, and the value (relative prices) of securities will adjust accordingly over time.

For example, in 1999 when Intel indicated that the company would not meet analysts' estimates for the upcoming earnings period, the price of the stock cracked and settled about 10 points lower. Over the next few days, analysts, traders, fund managers, and retail investors alike digested the news and made buy/sell decisions representative of the new paradigm for that stock. The addition of this new information caused a "rethinking" effect for the future earning potential of Intel Corporation. The price of the stock, which is based on a multiple of expected future earnings, was adjusted to reflect this shift.

As a secondary reaction to this news, related stocks in the computer hardware sector (such as DELL and CPQ) underwent paradigm shifts of their own and adjusted in price over the course of a week or so. To a lesser degree, a tertiary effect occurred in more distantly related stocks (such as COMS and CSCO).

The lag or time delay that exists between the primary, secondary, and tertiary ripple effect varies from sector to sector and is directly correlated to the magnitude and severity of news introduced into the existing paradigm.

To effectively add this concept to your basket of trading strategies, careful study, research, and diligent attention are required. Paradigms are constantly shifting, and each shift will affect the degree of magnitude and the time frame of the next paradigm shift. By keeping a close eye on the market and the way in which the sum total of all market participants react to news, a trader can effectively and accurately predict the degree and time frame in which various pieces of breaking news will affect the markets.

There are many repetitive news releases that will cause similar reactions by market participants. Earnings releases that meet, exceed, or fail to meet analysts' expectations are almost always cause the same reactions. The variance between the estimated and the actual earnings per share will determine the magnitude of reaction. The time frame in which the adjustment is made is almost always immediate and dramatic (i.e., a 40 point drop in stock price from one day to the next).

Secondary information that companies release with their quarterly earnings will be digested over varying periods of time. Secondary information can be the release of new products, market penetration, or adjustments in corporate expectations for future earnings periods. Because the net result of these secondary releases is not written in stone like an earnings release is, it leaves quite a bit of room for speculation and interpretation of the news over time.

Using a basic calculator, anyone can figure out the exact percent by which a company exceeded or failed to meet earnings. (However, when a company releases information that may affect the future earnings of the firm, an expanse of variables exist, and complex interpretation and extrapolation of possibilities is necessary.) There is a lot of room for speculation when interpreting the net result of uncertain future events. Therefore, the opinion of the masses will largely vary. Additionally, it takes a considerable amount of time to interpret, analyze, and incorporate such news. Therefore, the "adjustive" effect of such news is digested over a period of days, weeks, and months. Once the news has been fully digested by all market participants it can be considered "incorporated," and the resulting price of the security will reflect the average interpretation of the masses.

Even more reasonably reliable and stable piece of "repetitive" news are upgrades and downgrades. Different broker dealers and organizations continuously rate and rerate stocks. Within these organizations are analysts who are responsible for researching and reporting their findings. As with all news, the effect/degree of magnitude that various analysts/organizations have on stocks (and the overall market in general) varies considerably. Some analysts and organizations are notorious for releasing unreliable information, while others are consistently accurate in their predictions. The effect of their opinions, once made public, will impact the market accordingly.

As a rule of thumb, market participants have very short-term memories. An analyst or organization that has repeatedly made bad calls is sent down to the minor leagues and is not heard from again until he starts hitting homers. Usually, three or four homers in a row are enough to get drafted back into the major league. Once the attention of the media is focused on this player, the impact of his or her recommendations carries a great deal of weight when dropped in the public eye. The impact will often be significant and immediately acted upon by market participants.

To capitalize on analysts' and organizations' ratings of different stocks and sectors, traders must diligently research and gauge the impact of these groups and individuals. Who's hot this week?...this month? Who is everyone listening to? Who just made the cover of

Investors Business Daily, The Wall Street Journal, and Barron's? The story is there. All it takes is time, patience, and research to find it.

Another paradigm shift is caused by global conditions. For the majority of public companies, global occurrences do not have a profound effect on their condition and potential. This is not to say that there is no effect, but the effect will most likely not cause the dramatic short-term volatility that is so popular to the DayTrader. There are, however, a large number of globally oriented companies (such as IBM, GE, Gillette, and Intel) that react quite strongly to global events.

Any event that will affect the economy of a country responsible for five percent or more of a particular company's revenue will cause short to intermediate-term price movements. The degree to which a particular stock is dependent on the economy in question, and magnitude of the news, will determine the price movement. News that is highly speculative, or that takes a long period of time to take effect, is typically dismissed and causes little (if any) short-term price movement.

As with any business venture...

Some luck does exist. However, if luck is your strategy, Las Vegas is only a plane ride away. On the other hand, if you are looking for the consistent upper hand, you will have to pay the price of time spent doing your homework. The ace of spades is somewhere in the deck. Do you have the patience to count the cards, or are you the type that believes lady luck is on your side? The choice is yours. The decision you make will determine how fat or thin your wallet is.

To effectively implement this strategy, quite a bit of homework is required. I would suggest picking a handful of normally volatile stocks and researching where their revenue is derived. Keep this information in the back of your mind, and wait for the trade to materialize. This type of information is watched closely by professional analysts and fund managers, and it can cause substantial paradigm shifts that can last days or weeks. The elephant plays in this arena, and the potential for large profits can be found here (if you know what to look for). As with sector rotation analysis, start with 5 or 10 stocks. Learn them intimately. Trade them whenever the opportunity arises. Review your trades in these stocks, and watch the patterns closely. Take notes, be diligent, and remember to focus on just a handful of stocks to start.

19 SURGES AND CORRECTIONS

In a perfect world, news releases and the activities of market participants would be evenly distributed over time, and price reaction would occur solely on the magnitude of EACH release and/or action of institutional money managers. In the real world, however, news and institutional money rotation are not evenly distributed. The result of this "real world" action is that prices will sometimes "react" to a "compounded" number of variables over a very short period of time. In some instances, market participants overreact, causing a surge or correction in the market.

In a "normal" graph of a stock's price, there are two variables: price and time. Depending upon current sector and broad market conditions, in conjunction with company-specific news and money flow, stocks will shift in price over varying periods of time. Given these different variables, and the time frame in which these variables come into play, the variance or volatility of a stock's price will change at different rates over time.

For the following example, let's assume that every new variable introduced carries equal weight. Half of the variables are bullish on a given stock, and the other half are bearish. All of the information is released simultaneously. Given these assumptions, the ensuing price move will be reflected in a sideways movement in the stock's price. The time frame over which this pattern presents itself will depend upon how long it takes for all market participants to absorb the information.

In the next scenario, all of the variables carry different weights. Half the variables are bullish and half are bearish. In this case, the ensuing price movement will be representative of the sum total of all the weighted bullish variables less the sum total of all of the weighted bearish variables. Because these variables are not equally weighted, and because the weight of these variables is subject to interpretation by all market participants, the end result will be more difficult to determine. If all market participants place a net bearish bias on the sum total of these variables, the ensuing price movement will be bearish. However, due to the fact that these variables are subject to interpretation, the ensuing price movement will typically be quite jagged.

Consider a presidential election. In the New Hampshire primary, no candidate has won or lost in any state. Sure, there are opinion polls that give voters an indication of the outcome of the primary. However, there is no quantifiable information to prove the outcome of the election until all of the votes are counted. Therefore, voters tend to be more objective (relatively speaking) and pay closer attention to the candidates themselves and what each stands for (or appears to stand for). After the New Hampshire primary, there is clearly a leader in the presidential race. From that point forward, voters weigh not only the candidate and what he or she stands for, but also the opinions of the citizens that have already cast their votes (opinions).

In the stock market, information is released, and the fastest market participants react first (the first ones to the polls). Once market participants have reacted, the opinion is out, and the rest of the herd now has the new information (as well as the sentiment of the fastest market participants) to evaluate. Given this phenomenon, once new information is released into the marketplace, the initial weight of the information is further compounded by the market's display of public opinion. In fact, it is reasonable to say that charts are no more than public opinion polls. In the same way that people jump on the bandwagon in political elections, market participants have a propensity to do the same.

So far, we have assumed that all new information is released simultaneously, that half of the information is bullish, half is bearish, and that the weight of this information may or may not be equal. Now let's bring this picture into the real world. All information is not released simultaneously, and new information is not always half bullish and half bearish. With three different variables to consider (time, bias, and weight), it is sometimes very difficult to interpret the reaction that the sum total of all market participants will have.

In the real world, the net result of these variables can be dramatic. Whether you are considering a particular stock, sector, or broad market average, the sum total of all new information will cause varied degrees of price reaction over time. For example, when a large amount of very negative (positive) information is released into the marketplace at one time, the ensuing price move may result in a correction (surge [a.k.a., bull run]). Once the ball starts rolling, the "bandwagon" effect further compounds the movement. The "Asian Flu" correction in October 1997 is a perfect example of the impact that this phenomenon can have.

In the 1997 correction, market participants realized during the second trading day of the correction that, as a whole, they had overreacted and sent the market back up a few hundred points during the course of the day. This is a perfect example of how the "crowd" mentality works. It is similar to watching a large flock of birds circling around in the sky. They all fly in one direction, and then abruptly they all shift in another direction. I doubt that one bird is calling the shots. More likely, once a number of birds change course, the rest follow.

In addition to an onslaught of new information flooding the market, the "current market environment" is a variable that will affect the weight of new information. For example, let's assume that the market is very bullish, and the vast majority of information released into the marketplace in the prior weeks and months was also bullish. If an onslaught of bearish information is dumped into the public eye tomorrow, the current bullish environment of the market will offer support to offset the negative news. However, if the new information dumped on the market is also bullish, it will further confirm the present environment, and a bull run will ensue.

When waves of information combine, the effect is either a "neutralization" or "amplification" of the information. The degree to which the information is neutralized or amplified depends on the "power" of such information. This "action" is the basis for surges and corrections.

Waves of information can be compared to radio waves. When two radio waves combine with the peaks and troughs occurring at the same time, the height of the combined wave will equal the sum of the two waves. Furthermore, it is a rule of physics that there is no "perfectly efficient machine" and that energy dissipates over time. Information works the same way. (As a rule of thumb, the older the information, the less energy/weight it will carry in the current market.) The energy, or weight, that information carries dissipates over time. New information, like a radio wave coming out of a transmission tower, is fully charged and is received with clarity. As it travels through the air, the wave begins to weaken until it can no longer be picked up.

Waves, depending upon their strength and alignment with other waves, will affect the market differently. As a trader, you must always have your antennas up to receive and decipher these waves and mentally "database" the information. This database is then used as the basis to decipher and interpret new waves of information. Because new traders have a limited database, they are not able to receive and interpret these waves as effectively as experienced traders. This is precisely why most experienced traders earn more than less experienced traders. Experienced traders are better receivers and interpreters of new information.

20 SHARP MOVES IN THE MARKET... WHAT TO DO

During very bullish or very bearish days, a great deal of money can be made or lost. When the market is moving like a freight train, the worst thing a trader can do is step in front of it. Remember, the trend is your friend. Don't fight it. If the market is surging, go long. If it is tanking, go short. Don't try to pick bottoms or go against the prevailing trend unless a clear, substantiated reversal has materialized. (Note that trading retracements is a viable strategy...just not during incredibly strong moves in the market.)

Even during the most dramatic moves in the market, retracements occur. Many traders get faked out by these temporary "breaks" in the trend. Often, the stall or reversal is dramatic, and it looks very similar to a change in trend. However, if the market is moving sharply in one direction based on specific news, chances are that it will continue. One reason to believe that a stall is actually a reversal is if it is confirmed by breaking news that caused failure of the existing trend.

When a sharp trend stalls or retraces, your best bet is to lighten up your position and wait for confirmation of a top or bottom in the trend. If the trend has topped or bottomed out, it is time to close the trade. If the stall or retracement was just that, a stall or retracement, size back into your position when the trend resumes. If you are short stock, be careful about lightening up your position or liquidating on a stall or retracement. If the market is very bearish, you are lucky to be short, and I would recommend staying there. Chances are that you have locked in a good profit and can afford to give back 40 percent or so before bailing out.

If the market is sharply down, look for stocks that are positive, neutral, or only slightly negative in comparison to other companies in their sectors. If a stock is fighting the trend, it is an incredibly strong indication that the stock is going to move if the market retraces. There are two advantages to playing stocks that are fighting the trend. First, there is a high probability that you will profit from the trade. Second, if you are already following the trend, adding a trend fighter to your open position puts you in a spread trade. As you know, spread trades help to offset market risk, and in a volatile market, you need all of the systemic risk mitigants that you can get.

If you are short stock, there is a third advantage. Because of the uptick rule, it is often hard to get short stock when the market is tanking. By putting on a spread trade, you can (sort of) trade out of your position without exiting it. The difference is that your risk is not completely mitigated when you spread trade. The good news is that you have not mitigated all of your profit potential. Therefore, the risk associated with initiating a spread trade (versus exiting your long position) is offset by the fact that you can still profit on the trade.

In addition to being great money-making days, days with strong market movements are great times to do some research and preparation. You will have the

124

opportunity to take note of which stocks are fighting the trend. When the market does turn, these stocks will most likely move. The best trend-fighting stocks to trade are those that have been trending strongly during the previous days/weeks. When the market surges or tanks, the trends in these stocks (if contrary to the broad market movement) will stall and then resume when the sharp broad market movement subsides. This phenomenon reveals the true colors of a stock. Don't take this revealing information lightly. It is very powerful, and it is one of the best indicators of price movement that I have ever seen.

One final note on the subject of strong market movements. Such market conditions are great opportunities to make a great deal of money. However, for those that are inexperienced, such market movements are a great opportunity to lose a great deal of money. If you have not previously been in the market during a strong move, perhaps you should consider sitting the first one out. Use the opportunity to learn and to prepare for the end of the movement. By identifying trend-fighting stocks during these moves, you will be in a good position to capitalize on relatively low-risk trades when the market settles down.

21 FADE THE TRADE

There is an old adage about the market that goes something like this: "When mom and pop decide to get in, it is time to get out."

In other words, when the story hits mass publication, and the herd of retail investors begin shifting their money into the stock du jour, the buying opportunity is often past (or soon to be so). Unfortunately for the retail investor, he/she is usually the last to know what is going on in the market. Although this adage does not hold true for all retail investors, it is true to a high degree for the masses in general.

The question you are probably asking now is, "If this is true, then how can retail investors ever profit from the stock market?" The answer is that, over time, the stock market has an upward bias. The odds are in favor of making money. How much money one makes is the variable. If your average investor were to buy an S&P 500 Index fund, he/she would make an annual return of "X" percent. Had an investor bought the S&P 500 Index in 1995, he/she would be roughly twice as rich three years later, based on a compounded rate of return.

If this same investor picked stocks on his or her own, he/she might have either beaten the S&P or fallen short of it. Even if the investor beat the S&P, the relative risk that he/she took to lock in a greater return may have outstripped the return itself. For example, if an investor goes to Las Vegas each year with $100,000 to play a maximum of two hands of blackjack as his annual investment strategy, he is taking on considerable risk. Let's say that the investor gets blackjack on the first $100,000 hand. He wins $150,000. Then, on the second hand, he bets $100,000, busts, and goes home. For the year, the investor made a 50 percent return on his capital, which is pretty good by any standard. However, the risk that he took to realize that return far outstripped the realized return.

Given retail investors' limited access to information and the time delay in which information is conveyed to them, the fast money and the big money have often already taken their profits and moved on to greener pastures by the time the retail herd decides to get in.

By reading popular trade publications, and listening to the news that the average investor might use as a source of information, a DayTrader can make some reasonable assumptions as to what the retail herd is doing. This is not really a trading strategy, nor is it something that a DayTrader can really capitalize on on an intraday basis. However, it is a good forward-looking indication of things to come.

One way to fade the trade on an intraday basis is to watch closely for what I call the "DayTrader Effect." Simply put, it is reasonable to assume three things about DayTraders:

- DayTraders trade in 1,000 share lots.
- DayTraders don't like to take losses over 1/2 point.
- DayTraders trade off of CNBC.

Given these basic assumptions, the savvy DayTrader can watch the tape, watch the charts, and watch CNBC to "see" what the herd of DayTraders is doing. When a stock hits the news, and is followed by a massive number of 1,000-share prints on the time of sales, chances are very high that DayTraders are playing the stock. Watch carefully for which 1,000-share prints are at the bid price and which are at the ask price. Since short selling is not as popular amongst DayTraders as going long is (and because very few people will short a stock after a positive news break comes out on it), it is safe to assume that if the print is at the bid, a DayTrader is selling the stock. It is also safe to assume that if the print is at the ask, a DayTrader is buying the stock. Add up the buys and sells and you can determine what percentage of the cumulative daily trading volume is outstanding in the hands of DayTraders.

For example, when a stock begins to retrace and 1,000-share prints start hitting the bid in numbers (and the stock begins to downtick rapidly) get ready to buy. This is a sign of market makers trying to shake out the DayTraders. Depending upon the stock, market makers will sell for about half a point before buying back in and letting the stock continue to run. While this is happening, keep watching the prints at the bid. What you will notice, in many cases, is that the majority of 1,000-share prints that originally occurred at the ask have now printed at the bid. This means that the DayTrading herd has effectively been whipsawed out of the stock. Once the stock upticks twice, go long.

There is one caveat to this strategy. If the market has turned, and all stocks in that sector are fading at the same pace, it is probably not the best time to get in. You know that the stock has a bullish bias, that the stock has moved strongly to the upside, and that this particular stock is on the radar screens of hundreds (if not thousands) of traders. Be patient. Wait until the market turns to the upside, and then buy. Start with your standard share size, and then add to the position as it moves back up. Keep adding to the position in lots that are 1/4 to 1/2 the size of your normal trade size. Accumulate the stock until it is about 1/4 point from the high for the day, and then cash out.

This is a time tested strategy that works 70 percent of the time for me. Once you have established an initial profit, you are padded to some degree from a net loss on the trade. Adding to your position on a stock that has a strong bullish bias and has retraced with the broad market can be incredibly profitable. Remember, the market as a whole is often far stronger than an individual stock, even if there is incredibly positive news on that stock. Seize the opportunity to buy dips on strong stocks. The risk is low, and the return can be very high. Adding to gainers adds risk to the trade, so be careful.

22 ECONOMIC NEWS

    Alan Greenspan, head of the Federal Reserve, has by far more influence on the financial markets than any other individual. His every word and action is followed by the vast majority, if not all, of institutional market participants. The slightest hint that Greenspan is even considering a rate hike (or some other change in fiscal policy) is enough to cause dramatic reactions in the market. It was not too long ago that Greenspan uttered two words that caused the market to go into a tailspin that ended with a nearly 10 percent correction. Those two words, as most of you know, were "irrational exuberance." So powerful were these words that a shock wave began in the U.S. financial markets (equities, bonds, futures, etc.) and quickly spread around the globe.

    Greenspan and his crew rely on a multitude of economic reports and forecasts to keep inflation in check. There are a handful of indicators that Greenspan is quite fond of. He places greater weight on them as clear indications of times to come.

Gross National Product

    By far the most popular of Greenspan's forecasting

tools is Gross National Product. This is the broadest measure of economic activity, and thus it is the most important.

So, what is the GNP? The GNP is the sum total of all goods and services produced by the United States. This can also be stated as a measure of supply and demand for goods and services produced in the United States. Given that the expansion and contraction of the economy is based on the supply and demand for goods and services, the GNP provides valuable insight as to the direction the U.S. economy is moving. The GNP is also an excellent predictor of future economic conditions, because the growth of most companies is directly related to overall supply and demand.

There is one drawback to using the GNP as a forecasting tool; the GNP figure is published on a quarterly basis. Because of the time delay between releases, market participants must use other tools to anticipate the next quarterly figure. Almost all other economic indicators provide information about the GNP, and as a result they are used as GNP forecasting tools. The GNP is revised during the last week of each month, but less weight is placed on GNP revisions than the quarterly GNP report.

GNP is composed of Consumption (C), Investment (I), Government Purchases (G), and Net Exports [exports (X) minus imports (M)], or:

$$GNP = C + I + G + (X - M)$$

The most heavily weighted component of GNP is Consumption, which represents better than half of the

GNP. This is followed by Investment, then Government Purchases, and finally Net Exports (which is almost always a negative figure).

When the GNP figure comes in above estimates, bond prices fall and equity prices rise. There are rare exceptions to these rules, but for the most part they hold true. The reason for this is that a high GNP figure is a long-term indicator of inflation. Therefore, interest rates on bonds will increase (which means that the price of bonds will fall to reflect this). The stock market will typically react positively to this news, because higher GNP means a healthy economy in the short-term and thus higher sales and higher profits. HOWEVER, if inflationary fears are abound in the market, and a high GNP figure is released, equity prices will fall in reaction to these inflationary fears.

A side note...

... on the relationship of corporate growth to overall supply and demand. When there is competition for goods and services, supply and demand pressures apply. However, in the case of products and services that are monopolized by one company (or by a select few companies), supply and demand as forecasting tools are less useful. (This is not to say that they are not useful at all, but to a lesser degree.) Also, when a company provides a product or service that is absolutely essential, regardless of the price, supply and demand become far less useful as forecasting tools. When the price for a good or service has no correlation to supply and demand, it is known as "inelastic" to demand. A perfect example of this is insulin. Because diabetics must have insulin to live, they are willing to pay any amount for it.

> Fortunately, for diabetics, there are many suppliers of the drug. Consequently, competition keeps prices in check.

Employment

On a monthly basis the most valuable indicator is Employment. This indicator is broken down into four major categories: the unemployment rate, jobless claims, average hourly wages, and hours worked. Employment figures are released in the first week of every month, and they give the first "real" look at the economy. These figures help set the tone for the coming weeks.

Greenspan feels very strongly that the root of inflationary (or non-inflationary) pressures resides in people. I agree completely. As he explains it, if the unemployment rate is too low, and demand for workers outstrips the supply of workers, employers will have to offer higher wages to keep current employees and bring in new employees. The effect of this is twofold.

The first reaction to this paradigm is that employees are earning more. If employees earn more, then they have more money to spend, which results in increased demand for goods and services. Although competition keeps prices in check to a certain extent, over-demand and under-supply will eventually cause prices to go higher. Higher prices translate into less goods and services that a person can buy with a dollar. This can also be stated as decreased buying power of the dollar, or inflation.

The second reaction is on the side of the companies that have raised wages. Because employees can immediately go out and spend their excess income (while businesses typically react slower to such circumstances), inflationary pressure begins with the consumer and is further compounded by businesses over a period of time.

One might contend that if consumers are paying more for goods and services, employers will make more from each consumer, and thus there will be no need for businesses to raise prices. This is sometimes the case. Other times, and more often than not, retailers are the first to profit from this paradigm shift. Given inventories, purchasing contracts, etc., there is a lag time between the unbalancing of supply and demand by the consumer and the potential price reaction from manufacturers.

Because the consumer is at the root of the economy, the employment figures are a true forecasting tool for all other indicators. If you know how many people are employed and how much they earn, then you can roughly determine what they will be spending in the coming months. Therefore, car sales, housing starts, construction, retail sales, etc., will have a strong correlation to the employment figures. A highly divergent number will cause increased volatility in the marketplace, which is why it is crucial for DayTraders to fully understand and closely monitor the employment figures. You do not want to get blindsided by an employment report, and if you don't pay careful attention to them, it will eventually happen.

Retail Sales

One of the best forecasting tools available to interpret what the consumer is doing is the Retail Sales Report. This report is released during the second week of the month and is a reliable indicator of consumer spending. Remember, consumer spending (consumption) is the largest component of the GNP, and thus it carries a big stick in terms of how market participants react to it.

A strong retail sales figure is typically bullish for stocks, especially for the retail sector. When this figure is released, any variance from the estimate will cause retail stocks to react. It is a great trading opportunity, because the movements are sometimes large and tend to exhibit continuing trends for large potential gains. As with most trading strategies and opportunities, there are caveats. The caveat for the retail sales figure is that it is very hard to estimate and is subject to substantial revisions. Regardless, when a figure is released, it is usually taken as fact, not fiction, and remains so until revisions are released. If you are in a position in the retail sector, keep a watchful eye out for revisions, and adjust your position accordingly. You may want to lighten up on your position or close it out altogether in anticipation of a revision. If the revision is in your favor, you may consider adding to your position. Also consider adding a trade in a related stock in the same sector as an alternative, potentially less risky, diversified strategy.

Consumer Price Index

Another highly regarded measure of inflation is the Consumer Price Index. The CPI is a measure of the price of a fixed basket of goods and services at the consumer level. The CPI is an index with a base value of 100 (also known as abase 100 index). This index is currently based on the average price level of a fixed basket of consumer goods and services during the 1982-1984 period. By comparing the CPI index from two different time periods, a clear indication of value (or relative price level) can be determined.

Since the CPI is a <u>near-term</u> inflationary indicator, a CPI figure exceeding analyst estimates will typically be reacted to negatively by equity and bond market participants. Remember, when inflation rears its ugly head, the Fed positions itself to cool the economy down. Although no immediate action is taken in many cases, the sentiment of market participants is adjusted to reflect the predicted actions of the Federal Reserve (a.k.a., Alan).

There is some disagreement among analysts as to whether producers or consumers play a larger part with regard to inflation. The debate is not which group causes inflation, but rather, which came first, the chicken or the egg. Some analysts believe that producers are the first cause of inflation. Others believe that it is the consumer (and others believe that it is the Democrats). Nevertheless, all analysts agree that both the consumer and the producer make up the majority of the inflationary pie.

Producer Price Index

The first peek at inflation that traders will get each month at the producer level is the Producer Price Index, which is released in the second week of each month. The PPI measures prices at the producer level, and it measures the raw commodities that are used to produce consumer goods. There are three levels of production that are measured in the PPI: crude materials, intermediate goods, and finished goods. By measuring prices at various stages in the production process, a clear picture of overall prices can be established.

A PPI figure that comes in above estimates is a near-term inflationary indication and will cause a bearish reaction in both the bond and equity markets. When interpreting this indicator, it is important to remember that the PPI is also a base 100 index. As an index, it is often reported as an annualized rate. With this interpretation, the variance of the PPI can be quite high. The best way to interpret this indicator is to look at the PPI numbers over the past few months and compare. This will give you a much better picture of its relative weight or value.

Personal Income and Consumption Expenditures

An indicator that affects both the CPI and the PPI is Personal Income and Consumption Expenditures. Simply put, if you don't have money, you can't spend it. Thus, if you know how much consumers are making AND how much they are spending, you can predict with reasonable accuracy bow the PPI and CPI will be affected in the long run (given the correlation between consumer consumption [demand] and price levels).

Unlike the CPI and the PPI, growth in Personal Income and Consumption Expenditures is not necessarily inflationary in the short-term. Therefore, more disposable income is interpreted as a good sign in the equity markets, given that consumers with excess cash will be more inclined to spend and thus fatten the profits of companies. However, in the long term, continued growth in this area may cause inflationary pressures. If the market is fearful of inflation when this report is released, a negative reaction to a positive

Personal Income and Consumption Expenditures figure will ensue.

Index of Leading Economic Indicators

As a frontrunner (or early warning system for inflation), the Index of Leading Economic Indicators is used by almost all economists and analysts. The LEI is composed of 11 components:

- Average workweek in the manufacturing sector
- Building permits
- Change in unified orders
- Index of consumer expectations
- Initial unemployment claims
- New orders for consumer goods
- Plant and equipment orders
- Real M2
- Sensitive material prices
- Stock prices
- Vendor performance

Each of these components has equal weight. Combined, they paint an overall "macro" picture of the economy. As a general rule, three consecutive movements in the LEI in the same direction indicate that the economy is moving (or will move) in that direction. Since 1952, the LEI has "predicted" 10 recessions, but only seven have actually occurred. Still, an indicator that is 70 percent accurate is an incredible indicator. When analyzing the LEI report, it is important to keep in mind that the greatest reaction of market participants will occur on the third "confirming" report. Therefore, when the previous two reports are both bearish (or bullish), the third report will be watched closely by all. If the third report confirms the first two bearish reports, there is a 70 percent possibility that a recession will ensue, and the market will react accordingly.

Analysis of Economic Indicators

There are many other economic indicators that are watched by the Federal Reserve and market participants alike. These include The Beige Book, Consumer Sentiment, and the Merchandise Trade Balance. Depending upon current market conditions and sentiment of market participants, these indicators can carry different weights and cause varied reactions in the marketplace. To understand how the market reacts to economic news, you will need to closely monitor all reports. Over time, you will build up a mental "database" of economic indicators and the magnitude of the ensuing reactions to the releases of economic information.

Economic indicators are cumulative, meaning that one indicator confirms or negates the next. During periods when half of the indicators point in one direction and half point in the opposite direction, reactions in the marketplace will be less dramatic. During periods where the scale is tipped clearly in one direction or the other, economic news releases will cause substantial reactions in the marketplace. The degree to which the market will react depends upon the variance between estimated and actual figures.

For example, in July of 1996, the economic indicators poured in with inflationary sentiment one after another. The Federal Reserve publicly commented that it was considering raising interest rates, and the market got spooked. Each time a report was released with an inflationary bias, the market would crack to the downside. Each time a contrary indicator was released, the market would go up. Depending upon the indicator, and the variance of actual versus estimated figures, these swings were sometimes dramatic and far-reaching.

Different sectors of the market react to economic news with varying degrees of magnitude over varying periods of time. Some lead, some lag, and some do nothing. The Banking sector is always the first to react, because the earnings of banks are directly correlated to the economy and borrowing rates. The next sectors to react are those containing heavily debt-laden companies, such as the Transportation index, the Utility index, and the Paper index. If the Banking sector reacts too quickly for you to capitalize on an economic news release, look to these other sectors for trading opportunities. They move on economic news, but they tend to react slower than the banking sector. If you enter a trade in one of these sectors, use the Banking sector as a leading indicator of price movement for the sector that you are trading in. If you are trading in the Banking sector, use bonds as a leading indicator. There is a direct correlation.

Daytraders thrive on volatility. Second to earnings season, there is no other aspect of the equities market that causes as much volatility as do economic indicators. Therefore, it is of paramount importance that you, as a DayTrader, follow these figures with extreme diligence. If you do you will make more money. If you don't you will lose more money. The choice is yours.[3]

23 EARNINGS SEASON

Four times every year there exists an excellent opportunity to capitalize on corporate earnings. Between earnings periods, stocks will (in the absence of contrary broad market moves or contrary stock or sector-specific news) trend toward a price commensurate with the anticipated earnings in the upcoming quarter (given a PE Ratio comparable to the rest of the companies in the same industry group). During the month before the onslaught of earnings releases, traders, fund managers, and investors alike begin to worry about whether or not companies will meet or exceed their estimated earnings. Some traders, investors, and fund managers will play it safe and exit trades that they had been playing in anticipation of strong earnings. They will then reposition themselves in safer, less volatile stocks, in cash, or in a combination of the two.

As companies begin to report earnings, the market takes note. Closely related stocks will exhibit stronger correlations to each other. A strong earnings release in one stock will be followed by a strong price movement in correlated stocks. When larger, more "key" companies (such as Intel, Microsoft, IBM, and Ford) begin releasing or pre-releasing earnings or expected earnings, the secondary price reactions in related stocks become significant.

By paying close attention to which stocks are positively and negatively correlated to announcements of key companies, you can determine what the sentiment in the marketplace is for related companies.

For example, if DELL reports poor earnings, and IBM and GTW decline in price alongside DELL, you can rest assured that the market as a whole is worried about the earnings of these companies. On the other hand, if CPQ surges in price or does not react negatively to the news on DELL, chances are that the market as a whole feels very positive about the expected earnings for CPQ.

Sometimes there is a lag in the time that it takes for a stock to react to the news in a correlated stock. For example, if there is no price reaction in CPQ within three to four days, it is time to watch CPQ very closely for trading opportunities. Lack of volatility in a historically highly correlated stock is often a telltale sign of an ensuing move. Increased trading volume in a sideways chart pattern is after confirmation of an ensuing price move.

Be careful. If CPQ is within a week of releasing earnings, I would recommend not taking any long positions. If you have $100,000 in margined buying power and buy $50,000 worth of stock, you are highly exposed in an undiversified position. If CPQ pre-releases poor earnings while you are long the stock, you will be in big trouble. On the short side, however, the downside risk is comparably less. If CPQ pre-releases better than expected earnings, the price of the stock will not "crack" to the upside. It may spike up a few points and continue higher, but a 30 percent to 50 percent immediate upside price move is quite unlikely. On the other hand, if CPQ pre-releases poor earnings, such a price move is highly probable. Therefore, it is safe to say that going long a volatile stock during earnings season is far riskier than going short.

By concentrating on the short side during earnings season, not only can you capitalize on intraday retracements (when the time is right), you can also "luck" into aberrations which can yield huge gains. For the most part, I would not recommend playing stocks that are within a week of releasing earnings, unless at least 75 percent of the planets appear to be aligned in your favor.

If you do feel the need to play on the long side during earnings season, consider spread trading a positively correlated stock with a rating of roughly 0.5 that exhibits a lag time in price movement. This will dramatically reduce your risk exposure. These opportunities are relatively easy to identify. Although the returns associated with spread trading positively correlated stocks are lower than those just going long, the risk associated with the trade is dramatically reduced.

During earnings season, I strongly recommend not spread trading negatively correlated stocks. If either stock comes out with a pre-release that is contrary to the position you took in the stock, you will get nailed on both sides of the trade. This can be disastrous, especially if you have allocated a large portion of your buying power to this strategy.

During earnings season, I strongly recommend not holding overnight positions. This can be very dangerous on both the long and short side. If you do feel the need to hold overnight positions during earnings season, you should have a very, very, very good reason for doing so. Even with such a reason, I would suggest holding a smaller than normal position to lessen the risk of a disastrous aberration.

The risk that DayTraders often take during earnings season is sometimes disproportionate to the potential reward. If you are new to DayTrading, I suggest riding the bench the first time around. One bad move could put you seriously in the hole or even out of business. Give yourself the luxury of time to learn about earnings season before you risk your new profession to make a few bucks. It is not worth it. There are quite a few thorns that can prick you in the eye during earnings season. If you don't know where you are going, you stand a much higher chance of running straight into one of those thorns.

For experienced traders, do what you do best. Play the strategies that have worked for you in the past, and keep your relative risk exposure as low as possible. Here's where your months and years of homework can really pay off.

As you may already know, it is crucial that you pay extremely close attention to the markets during earnings season, and watch the news closer than ever. Step up the pre- and post-market research. Seek first to understand and then to capitalize. Having been through a number of earnings periods, you now know what thorns to look out for. Stick to what you know, and begin looking for new opportunities that you can implement three months from now.

Earnings season should be viewed as a time first to learn and second to make money. As you gain more experience, earnings season will evolve into periods of learning AND earning. The longer you stay in the game, the more trading opportunities you will learn about. If you get overzealous during your first earnings season, you may be watching the rest from the sideline. If you watch the first earnings season from the sideline, you may be pulling Club Med vacations and new cars out of the market quarter after quarter going forward. The choice is yours.

DayTrading into the Millennium

24 LEVEL II: A LEVEL BEYOND

The traditional quote system used by most retail investors only reveals the inside market, which is the highest bid and the lowest ask price for a given stock. These investors are at a distinct disadvantage to those who have Level II quotes, which not only reveal the inside market, they also reveal bids and offers above and below the inside market. With the advantage of being able to see how much supply (ask) and demand (bid,) exists for a given stock, a clearer "picture" of the probable price movement can be derived. Once a trader understands what to look for on the Level II screen, he/she can predict price movements more accurately.

Level II data shows which market makers or ECNs are bidding for/offering stock, the price, and the number of shares that are being bid for or offered. The more advanced trading platforms also include Time of Sales (TOS), which shows the quantity, price, and time at which trades have taken place. Some systems reveal which market makers and ECNs have been at the inside bid and ask the most times, second most times, third most times, etc. To fully understand the interaction of these different components, a detailed explanation is in order.

I will begin with Level II data. Pockets of supply and demand can be seen throughout the Level II screen. As you get farther from the inside quote, the reliability of the quotes generally becomes less. The reason for this is market makers often post bids and offers that they have little or no intention of honoring. One theory for this behavior is that the market maker is giving the "appearance" of supply or demand to "fake" support/resistance in favor of the firm's _true_ position. Of course, not all "far away" quotes are bogus. Many represent customer limit orders, which are true supply and demand. Within an eighth of a point of the inside quote, market maker bids and offers tend to be the most reliable. At the inside quote, the vast majority of market maker bids and offers are genuine. This is partly because of the SOES mandatory execution rule, which allows market makers at the inside quote to get "picked off" by traders using SOES. Therefore, market makers that are not interested in buying and selling typically "hang back" from the inside quote.

By understanding how market makers work, you can better predict their actions. Market makers can only do 12 things. Six are generally bullish, and six are generally bearish. (These actions are shown in Table 2.) By paying close attention to the actions of market makers, a trader can determine which market makers are "for real" and which are not.

There are many tricks that market makers employ to get traders off their scent. One trick is to continuously pull back the offer (bid) a level each time the ask upticks (bid downticks). This way the market maker is still "participating in the market" but is safe from getting picked off. If you notice a market maker doing this consistently, you can rest assured that he/she is not in the game today.

Another trick that market makers play is to show size in the "outside market" and then tick it closer to the inside quote to give the impression of aggressiveness. When a market maker does this, it is typically an indication of a low and away pitch...but always watch out for the pitch being "in your ear." Sometimes these actions are real, so beware. If the market maker gets close to the inside quote and stops short, his hand is played...low and away. In this case, it is reasonable to assume that the market maker is actually on the other side of the market and is attempting to give a false impression. Either that or he is bored and has nothing better to do at the moment.

However, if the market maker moves to the inside quote and starts buying shares, for example, then the pitch is "in your ear." This buyer is aggressive, and the size can be assumed to be genuine with relative confidence. You will not see this action too often, because market makers will do their best to hide their intention. In the rare instance that this pattern reveals itself, go with the flow. If the market maker is a seller, try to get short (although this will be very difficult to do if an aggressive seller is down-ticking the offer and "whacking" the bid). If the market maker is a buyer, buy. Since he is aggressive, you will have to leapfrog him. You can either split the spread using an ECN, take the offer, or bid above the offer on SNET for a higher probability of a fill. With an aggressive buyer at the inside quote, I would not recommend splitting the spread. Don't be cheap. There is a high probability that this trade will be successful, and it is a rare opportunity to make a low risk profit. Try to take the offer using

SOES. If there are too many buyers attempting to do the same thing that you are, cancel your order and broadcast a bid 1/16 above the inside offer to all market makers. There is a much higher probability of getting filled at a higher price than at the inside ask price, especially when there is an influx of buying pressure.

The risk associated with this trade is that a size seller is waiting in the wings and will hit the bid in size, eliminating the demand. If this happens, exit the trade immediately, and consider getting short. If a size seller reveals himself, he probably has more to sell.

If the market maker is a size buyer or seller of shares, another trick that he will often employ (sometimes in conjunction with the aforementioned trick) is to "hide" the size. For example, if the market maker is a size seller of stock, he may only reveal a small portion of the order. He will go to the inside ask, sell a few thousand shares, and then "reload" (refresh the ask). When those shares are taken, he will reload again ... and again ... and again. You will see these trades in the TOS. When you see a market maker reloading, there are a number of factors to consider. First, who is the market maker? If you have been watching the stock closely over the past days and weeks, you will have developed a feel for who the "key" market makers are in the stock. Is the market maker who is reloading a key player? If so, add more weight to this consideration. If he is not, take notice. It could be that the market maker only has a limited number of shares to offer and will soon be done selling. One way to quickly determine whether or not the market maker is a key player in a stock is to use the indicator that tells which market makers have been at the inside ask the most times during the day. If you do

Table 2. Twelve Market Maker Moves

DOWNSIDE MOVEMENTS	
Joins Ask	Market maker decreases its ask price to the inside ask
Leaves Bid	Market maker changes its price downward from the inside bid price
Refreshes Ask	Market maker sells at the ask and "refreshes" its price at the inside ask with additional shares
New Low Ask	Market maker quotes a lower ask than the rest of the market makers
Bid to Ask	Market maker leaves the bid and simultaneously joins the ask
Drops Bid	The last market maker at the inside bid decreases its price, thereby lowering the price of the inside bid
UPSIDE MOVEMENTS	
Leaves Ask	Market maker changes its price upwards from the inside ask price
Joins Bid	Market maker changes its price upward to the inside bid price
Refreshes Ask	Market maker buys at the bid and "refreshes" its price at the inside bid with additional shares
New High Bid	Market maker quotes a higher bid than the rest of the market makers
Ask to Bid	Market maker leaves the ask and simultaneously joins the bid
Lifts Ask	The last maker at the inside ask increases its price, thereby raising the price of the inside ask

not have this tool, I highly recommend that you switch to a platform that does have it. This is one of the most powerful decision support tools available, and one that you cannot afford to trade without.

By knowing which market makers have been at the inside bid and ask the most times, second most times, etc., you can quickly determine who the key players in a stock are. With this tool, you will be able to evaluate the relative weight that each market maker possesses in any stock. If a piece of news comes out on a stock that you have never heard of before, a quick glance at this decision support tool will reveal what takes traders days or weeks of close attention to determine. In conjunction with the aforementioned example, this tool can be used to further confirm supply and demand pressure in a stock and enable the trader to make a quick decision to act or not act. If a key market maker is reloading at the ask and other key market makers are right behind him, it is a clear indication of resistance to upward movement.

The next step is to evaluate the market makers on the bid side. Which market makers are at the inside bid? Are they key market makers? How much size are they bidding for? Is it far less than the size being offered? The answers to these questions will quickly reveal to the trader what action to take. (Remember, no action at all is an action in itself.) Unfortunately for the trader, when a market maker is reloading at the offer, it will be difficult to get short. If you can, great. If not, wait.

When the selling pressure subsides, the stock is likely to bounce back. Sometimes size sellers (buyers) will pause and allow the stock to retrace. Without the pause, the seller (buyer) will place too much continuous pressure on a stock and drive the price down (up) considerably. To avoid getting a lower dollar cost average price, the seller (buyer) will take a breather and let the action of market participants retrace the movement in the stock that was caused by the onslaught of selling (buying) pressure. This is a great opportunity to make an eighth, a quarter, or a half on the long (short) side, depending upon the volatility in the stock and the extent to which the selling (buying) pressure pushed the stock price down (up).

On the subject of key market makers, don't believe for a moment that they are all the same. Goldman Sachs (GSCO), Merrill Lynch (MLCO), Bear Sterns (BEST), Morgan Stanley (MSCO), and Solomon Smith Barney (SBSH) are widely known to be big players in the stocks that they make markets in. Not only do savvy traders follow their every move, other market makers do as well. In my opinion, GSCO is the most reputable, highly regarded, powerful market maker on the street. GSCO is not the key market maker in all stocks that it makes a market in. Nevertheless, when GSCO starts to get aggressive, everyone takes note. By paying close attention to GSCO's actions (number of times at inside quote, confirmation of trades on the TOS, the general movement of its bids and offers around the inside quote, etc.) a trader can develop a good "feel" for the movement of the stock. I cannot count the times that an action by GSCO has been followed by the same action by other market makers.

For example, if GSCO switches from ask to bid, other market makers will often follow suit. When this happens, many traders take note and often adjust their positions accordingly. Unfortunately, GSCO and other market makers are well aware of this and use this action to fake traders out. It is only by paying close attention that a trader can evaluate whether a savvy market maker is trying to fake you out. This is why having an indicator that reveals which market makers have been at the inside quote the most times is so important. It helps to show the market makers' true intention.

Once you know who the key market makers are, you can estimate potential levels of support and resistance. Typically, market makers will bid for and offer shares of the same stock at different levels. Therefore, it is important to look at the levels that market makers are grouping at. If key market makers are upticking the bid, and those same market makers are offering stock at a higher level, there is a high probability that some resistance will be met when that level is reached. Thus, if you are long the stock, plan an exit strategy a sixteenth below the resistance level. If you get greedy and try to sell your shares at the same level that the key market makers will likely be selling at, you may have a hard time exiting the trade...and wind up foregoing more than the sixteenth that you would have foregone by playing it safe.

When evaluating a trade, Level II analysis is one of five factors that a trader can use to make an informed decision. The other factors are:

- Time of Sales
- Technicals
- Sector Analysis
- Broad Market Analysis

TOS can be used to "see" block trades which do not show up on the Level II screen. Block trades by themselves sometimes mean nothing. Many times they are a one-time occurrence and will have no effect on the price of the stock. However, if a number of block trades go off at or near the same priced, they are a clear indication of large buying or selling interest in the stock. If a number of block trades occur below the bid, it is clearly selling pressure. If a number of block trades occur above the ask, it is clearly buying pressure.

Typically, if a gigantic block trade occurs, the pressure is history for the time being. Nevertheless, size buyers & and sellers are usually the most informed players, and large block trades are often an indication of events to come. When a number of large block trades occur in a stock, take notice. There is always a reason behind the action. In some cases, it is nothing more than repositioning of capital by a large player and is not indicative of underlying conditions. It also may be an insider diversifying his position a bit. This does not necessarily mean that the insider knows something that is about to occur. It could be that he is buying a new Jaguar XJ220S for $375,000 and needs some cash.

However, in some cases, block trades are indicative of times to come. To effectively evaluate the reason behind the trade, the trader needs to use his/her first investigative tool. Look at the actions of the key market makers. How are they reacting to the block trades? Are they upticking the bid?...switching from bid to ask?...refreshing the bid?...making a new low ask?

Next, you will need to look to the third of the five tools needed to effectively evaluate the "condition" of a stock: charts. The most advanced trading platforms have a function that allows the trader to "link" charts to the Level II box. By doing this, the trader can type in a stock symbol in the Level II box and immediately see the intraday and daily chart, as well as different technical indicators. For example, by linking four charts to the Level II box, a trader can see a candlestick, bar, tick-by-tick, and line chart at the same time. Depending upon the trading platform, the trader can also see technical indicators, such as overlays of other stocks, Bollinger Bands, oscillators, and moving averages. Without the chart linking function, a trader would have to type in the ticker symbol five times to get a complete "picture" of the stock. By the time a trader completes this action, the stock may already have moved one or two levels. Technical analysis is discussed in detail in "Technicals," Chapter 11 of this book, so I will not go into too much detail here. Use the "planetary alignment" technique described there to further evaluate the stock's condition.

If the technicals on the stock look good, the next step is to evaluate the sector that the stock trades in. Is the stock that you are considering convergent or divergent to the sector? Has this pattern existed for a number of days or weeks? Closely related stock and sector analysis can be effectively used to confirm (or not confirm) price movement in a particular stock. As a trader, you will need to determine what weight to give this analytical tool in conjunction with the other tools that you are utilizing. (This is more of an art than a quantifiable skill and can be acquired over time.)

Last, the trader needs to evaluate the condition of a stock in comparison to the broad market. The tick indicator, the futures, and the broad market averages themselves are the key tools in broad market analysis. Depending upon the stocks (bank and utility stocks, for example), bonds can also be used as a confirming indicator. I generally place less weight on the overall market trend if the trend is light. However, if there is sharp movement in the market, I place a heavy weight on this analytical tool. If the market is tanking, most stocks will follow the trend. And remember, don't fight the trend!

In addition to the planetary alignment technique used to evaluate technicals, it may be helpful to consider the five tools just discussed in terms of planetary alignment. There are large and small planets. Some have greater gravitational pull than others. The size and pull of planets are constantly changing, and differ from stock to stock and sector to sector. Experienced traders have an intuitive sense of the relative weight of different indicators in different environments. With enough determination and patience, almost anyone can develop a feel for the relative weight and pull of different indicators.

The hardest part about evaluating Level II and the movements and actions of market makers is that they are well aware of what you are trying to do. In this chapter, I have used the words "often," "typically," "sometimes," and "in some cases." These words are vague, indeed. The reason for this is that market makers are as vague as possible in their actions. They are continuously trying to cloak their actions and hide from you - the enemy. As soon as traders figure out what a market maker is up to, they make his life miserable. Therefore, the market maker is constantly bobbing and weaving to avoid detection. Market makers are chameleons, and only by paying close attention can you see them hiding in the canopy of illusion.

25 Holding Overnights

As a trader, I hold overnights. In fact, holding overnights is a strategy that I employ on a regular basis. Depending upon the security that I am trading and the current sector and market conditions, I sometimes feel that the trade that I am in is still ripe for profits. The decision to hold overnights is the sum total of quite a few variables. If 75 percent of the planets (and their moons) are in alignment, and the 25 percent that are not in alignment carry relatively little weight, I will choose to hold overnight.

The first and most heavily weighted planet is the stock itself. Regardless of whether I am long or short, I will never hold the position overnight if:

- The earnings are due to be released for a highly correlated company.
- The news surrounding the stock is not predominantly supportive of my position.
- The company is due to release earnings within the next month.
- I do not know the company intimately well.
- The graph on the stock shows strong resistance within a point of my current position.

- The graph shows a hint of weakness in relation to my position.
- The volume surrounding the price move that I am capitalizing on does not confirm the chart.
- The chart is displaying a sideways pattern.

There are a number of telltale signs that I look for in a stock when determining whether to hold overnight. Reasonably low volatility (no five plus point gap moves in the past six months) is of paramount importance to me. I am not one to take on excessive risk, and I consider the possibility of violent overnight price movements to be a little more than I prefer to handle. Further, I will only consider holding an overnight position if the stock is trending and is confirmed by increasing average daily volume. A reasonably low PE Ratio is also a consideration, but only when I have a long position. For overnight shorts, the higher the PE Ratio, the better I feel. If there is a supportive band of accumulation/distribution within a point of my position (within the last six months, although the more recent the better) I am the most comfortable. Finally, I look for stocks that have a tendency to gap open in the neighborhood of 3/4 of a point or greater. If a stock typically opens flat, I will pass on the overnight because I can most likely get in at the open and capture the same price move without the added risk.

The next planet that I consider, when deciding whether or not to hold a position overnight, is the sector that I am trading within. If the stock that I am trading has a highly negative correlation to the sector, then I will hold the position only if the sector is trending opposite my position.

The third planet that I consider is the broad market. I look to the broad market to a lesser degree than I do the particular sector that I am trading within. What I do take note of is the correlation between the sector and the broad market. If the sector is highly positively or negatively correlated with the broad market, I will only hold a position overnight if the broad market appears to be supportive of the sector (in relation to the position that I am holding). If there is no strong correlation between the broad market and the sector, then I pay very little attention to the broad market, if any.

The fourth planet that I consider is upcoming news that might affect the entire market. If key economic data is due to be released within three to four days, I will pass on overnights. If there is the potential for a tidal wave in California, a war in Russia, or some other significant event, I will again pass.

The final planet that I consider is the Federal Reserve. I will never hold an overnight position within seven days of a Fed meeting, unless at least 75 percent of all analysts don't believe that the Fed will act at the meeting. That being the case, I tend to ignore it.

As long as I know the stock that I am trading intimately well, I don't really care whether the trade is profitable or not at the end of the day — if I initiated the trade with the intention of holding it for an extended period of time. I am disciplined enough to exit a trade if it is a dud. I never consider holding an overnight because I don't want to take a loss. In my mind, the loss is taken tick by tick, regardless of whether I actually exit the trade or not. Kidding yourself that "a loss does not exist unless you exit the trade" is one of the most illogical things I have ever heard. If you ever consider holding an overnight position because you don't want to accept a loss, you need help.

26 TRIPLE-WITCHING

Triple-witching day is the third Friday of the month that ends each quarter. It marks the simultaneous expiration of stock options, index options, and index futures. Triple-witching is associated with increased market volatility. Stock options that are exercised (which translates into stocks being bought and sold) create substantial increases in trading volume. Because of the added volatility in the markets, the futures-to-cash premium experiences more frequent imbalances, resulting in the initiation of program trading. Additionally, many traders are attempting to unwind their positions or roll them over to the next expiration month. The simultaneous expiration of these fine contracts and the actions associated with them causes rapid, sometimes chaotic, fluctuations in the market.

Because the stakes are often very high in these contracts, sizeable intraday gains and losses can occur as these contracts approach expiration. For options traders, the optimal price of the stock at expiration will equal the strike price of the underlying option contract that they are most heavily concentrated in. Depending upon the size of the position that an options trader has, it is sometimes beneficial to try to move the price of the stock to the desired strike price by buying or selling large quantities of the stock. Because there are different strike prices, and options traders have varied positions at each of these strike prices, competition to move the stock to one strike price or another sometimes ensues. This competition translates into abnormal trading volume, in conjunction with increased volatility.

This competition occurs most often in stocks that have large outstanding options positions. Often the price of a stock will move right to the strike price and will close with an inside bid or ask price touching the strike price. The most volatile movement typically occurs in the last two hours of trading, when stocks start to "run" for the strike price. Depending upon the cross currents, a stock can near one strike price and then take an about-face and race to a strike price five points away. This does happen, so be very careful if you decide to trade on a triple-witching day.

A number of different tools can be used to determine whether or not a stock might run for a strike price (also known as "running for the money"). The first and easiest way is to scan through a list of stocks that have large outstanding interests in the underlying options contracts. (Some prep-work is required for this strategy.) Keep a close eye on your list of stocks, and scan them throughout the day. When you have identified a stock that could be a runner, look to the inside quote. You will often see large size at the bid or offer. Traders attempting to move the market to a particular strike price will show their muscle. By showing size at the inside quote, traders using this strategy hope to 1) scare off anyone thinking about going the other way, and 2) seek assistance from other traders looking to make a fast buck. By showing size, traders thinking about selling may hold off until the buying subsides, and vice versa. For DayTraders, size at the inside quote is a strong indication that the stock is going to move in a particular direction (as long as there is limited resistance on the other side of the inside quote). For over the counter securities, traders have the advantage of seeing which market makers are bidding for and offering stock. If one particular market maker is showing size and/or taking the offer and upticking the bid continuously, you can be quite confident of the reason behind his actions.

If you decide to take a position in a particular stock, don't take your eyes off it for a second. Triple-witching days are very unusual, and volatility is high. This strategy is risky, but the profit potential is high. When in this type of trade, set a low risk tolerance, and exit the trade immediately if it starts to go against you. You may wish to consider entering trailing limit and stop limit orders 3/8 behind your trade (note that stop orders are only available for listed securities). By continuously updating your limit or stop limit order you can lock in your profits and limit your losses. The downside to the use of limits and stop limits is that you might get "picked off" or "shaken out" of what otherwise would have been a profitable trade. Depending upon how far from the inside quote you set your limits or stop limits, you can reduce the risk of getting picked off or shaken out of a trade. However, the farther out that you put the trailing stops or limit orders, the higher your risk of larger losses.

When using a buy (sell) stop order, it becomes a market order only after a trade at or above (below) that price takes place. Thus, if a stock runs against you, the price that you get filled at may be less desirable than the stop price. If you use a buy (sell) stop limit order, it becomes a marketable limit order only after a trade at or above (below) that price takes place. Therefore, the market may run through your price without giving you a fill. If you use a limit order on an ECN like Island, the market may run through your price without giving you a fill. If this happens, you will be stuck at a higher price, and the market may continue against your position. Therefore, even limit and stop limit orders are by no means total insurance against sizeable losses.

Even more volatile than triple-witching days are the "quadruple-witching" periods, which occur every June. Each June, the Frank Russell Company reconfigures the Russell 2000 Index, which is a barometer for small-cap stocks. There is considerable added trading activity in stocks that are added to the index, as well as stocks that are de-listed from the index. Typically, index fund managers dump stocks that are de-listed from the Russell 2000 and buy newly listed stocks. However, in conjunction with triple-witching, very strange things can happen. Therefore, if you are taking advantage of the Russell 2000 listed/de-listed play, be very watchful and very careful. If the stock that you are trading starts running for the money in the direction of your trade, hold on. If it starts running against you, re-evaluate...quickly.

The best way to add the triple-witching strategy to your arsenal of trading strategies is to sit the next one out and take careful notes. Begin by compiling a list of stocks that have large underlying options positions. Watch these stocks closely throughout the day, and take notes on the actions that these stocks exhibit. What is the average daily trading volume in the stock? What is the daily trading volume during <u>this</u> day?

At the end of the day, you should also scan through as many different stocks as possible and identify those that ran for the money. If you can, print out the intraday and daily chart for each stock that fits this pattern, and save it for reference at the next triple-witching event. For Nasdaq stocks that ran for the money, note which market makers drove them there. Also note what the overall market did that day and what each sector did. Analyze the Ticks, the TRIN, and the futures, and attempt to identify patterns or telltale indicators.

With this arsenal of data you will stand a good chance of making money on the next triple-witching day. Remember, however, that it is crucial to use as many tools as possible when identifying trading opportunities. Just because a stock ran for the money during one triple-witching day does not necessarily mean that it will do it at the next. Caveat Emptor!

27 MARKET ON CLOSE

One extremely effective trading strategy I learned while trading in Manhattan was the "Market on Close" strategy. Before explaining the strategy I would like to first define exactly what a market-on-close (MOC) order is and the most important rules surrounding it. The rules described herein are not comprehensive and are subject to change, so be sure to check with your broker for the compete list of current rules before implementing this strategy.

The Exchange defines an MOC order as "a market order which is to be executed in its entirety at the closing price on the Exchange of the stock named in the order, and if not so executed, is to be treated as canceled." When there is an imbalance of MOC orders, the stock that represents the imbalance is executed against the prevailing bid or offer on the Exchange at the close of trading and sets the closing price. This means that an excess of MOC buy orders are executed against the offer, and an excess of MOC sell orders are executed against the bid. The remaining buy and sell MOC orders are paired off at the price at which the imbalance was executed. When the total size of the MOC buy orders equals the total size of the MOC sell orders, the buy and sell orders are paired off at the price of the previous NYSE trade. The result of these pricing procedures is that all executed MOC orders receive the same closing price. Executable limit orders in the Book may be left unfilled because the paired MOC orders are crossed rather than executed against the orders in the Book.

For example, at 3:59 p.m. the last trade in ABC was 30 1/8, and ABC is quoted at 30 bid for 800 shares, 600 offered at 30 1/4. MOC orders represent 1,000 to buy and 1,500 to sell. The 500 share imbalance is executed against the 30 bid and is reported on the Tape. The remaining 1,000 by 1,000 MOC shares are paired off, also at 30, and are reported on the Tape separately as "stopped stock." Had there been no imbalance in the MOC orders (the MOC orders would be 1,000 to buy and 1,000 to sell) they would simply have been paired off at 30 1/8, which was the last trade price and reported on the Tape as "stopped stock."

Every third Friday of each month, the stock market experiences a large surge in MOC orders associated with the expiration of several index derivative products. In order to facilitate the pricing of the large volume of expiration-related MOC orders, the NYSE has introduced special order-entry cancellation procedures. On monthly expiration days, no MOC orders in any stock can be canceled or changed after 3:45 p.m. Also, MOC orders relating to any strategy involving any index derivative product must be entered before 3:00 p.m.

To further facilitate the orderly representation of MOC orders, during monthly expirations the NYSE announces MOC order imbalances of 50,000 shares or more for a group of "pilot" stocks. The pilot stocks consist of the 50 New York Stock Exchange S&P stocks (with the highest market capitalization) plus any other component stocks of the of the Major Market Index. The imbalance announcements are disseminated (via the Tape) as soon as possible after 3:00 p.m., after 3:30 p.m., and again after 3:45 p.m. Once an imbalance announcement has been made, only MOC orders on the opposite side of the published imbalance are accepted. For pilot stocks with MOC order imbalances of less than 50,000 shares, a "no imbalance" notice is published, and thereafter no MOC orders are accepted. Finally, to increase the flow of information on non-expiration trading days, the NYSE disseminates (on every trading day) pilot stock MOC order imbalances of 50,000 shares or more as soon as possible after 3:45 p.m.

Now that I have explained the basics of MOCS I will explain the strategy. When the buy or sell imbalance is equal to or greater than 10 percent of the average daily trading volume in a stock, and the trend of the market complements the imbalance, go with the flow. If it is a buy imbalance that is being reported, buy the stock at the market, and enter an MOC order to sell the shares. If it is a sell imbalance that is being reported, try to get short. If you are successful at shorting the stock, enter an MOC order to buy the shares back.

My experience has been that this strategy works about 70 percent of the time. When it does not work, the imbalance almost always protects you from sizeable losses. On the losing trades, a loss of 1/16 to a maximum of 1/2 point is to be expected. For winning trades, profits range from an average of 1/4 point to a maximum of two to three points.

Because this is a high probability proposition that offers larger gains and smaller losses, I would recommend that everyone employ this strategy, However, it is important to first understand the risks. All MOC orders are not necessarily executed at the close, and reporting of executions sometimes does not occur until the next day. Again, ask your broker for a complete set of current rules pertaining to MOC orders, and study them diligently before implementing this strategy.[4]

28 PSYCHOLOGY OF DAYTRADING

Regardless of the amount of diligent research a DayTrader does, if he/she is not psychologically capable of making decisions based on probabilities and facts, he/she is destined to fail. In DayTrading, timing is everything. If you cannot time a trade correctly, you will lose money (or not make as much as you could have). If you place trades for any other reason than rational, carefully weighted and considered reasons, then you have crossed the line from disciplined businessman or woman clearly into the realm of the gambler (or the not-so-smart trader).

The mindset that you enter a trading day with will affect your trading decisions until your mindset changes. If you had a huge fight with your husband or wife 15 minutes before the open, you will have a propensity to bias the market on the downside. If you had a nice "morning interlude" with your significant other, you will most likely have a more positive outlook on the market. Of course this is not an absolute truth in all circumstances. For the most part, however, your mood will affect your trading mindset and the buy/sell decisions that you make. Be cognizant of your mood. Ask yourself, "Am I being objective, or am I pissed off at my dog for "violating" my $6,000 Oriental rug this morning?"

Knowing yourself and understanding your likes, dislikes, and idiosyncrasies will be a huge benefit to your trading results. If you can differentiate your personal psychology from the market, you will be far better prepared to interpret information, numbers, and facts objectively. You will also be able to effectively add to your statistical advantage (or lessen your lack thereof).

A ritual that I perform every day is to close my eyes and take 10 deep breaths. I attempt to clear my mind of all thoughts and focus on the sound of my breathing. Any thoughts that pass through my consciousness are allowed to drift by. I never fight to keep thoughts from my consciousness. I simply don't focus or expand on these thoughts. I let them drift by like clouds in the sky on a warm, breezy spring day. I picture myself on a beach in the Bahamas, my feet in the wet sand by the edge of the sea, and the sun shining down gently upon me. Blue waters, green palms, and a few scantily clad native women off in the distance.

For some, this may sound like a bunch of new-age crap. For me, it works. It helps me clear my head of the normal b.s. of life and helps to put me in an objective mindset. This works for me ... not just with regard to trading, but for life in general. Do what works for you.

During the trading day, I sometimes find myself exuberant or depressed over the preceding trades of the day. I find myself, on profitable days, looking for anything that I can find to trade. Sometimes I have an incredibly strong feel for the market. Sometimes I don't. On days that I can feel the pulse of the market as strongly as I can my own pulse after a five-mile run, I go with my instincts and don't hold back.

On days when I don't have a strong feel for the market, I act differently. If I am getting too excited, I will close my eyes and hold my breath for as long as I possibly can (my record is two minutes and 20 seconds). As silly as it sounds, the pain of burning lungs can bring you down to earth very quickly. I don't recommend this for people with heart conditions (nor do I recommend DayTrading for these types). For those of you in good physical health, try it. It just may work.

On days when I am depressed about the "learning experiences" that I have piled up, I try the pre-market breathing exercise first. If this doesn't work, I open my word processor and write about my bad trades. When the exercise works, I return to trading. When it does not, I take the rest of the day off and use the time to research. I am always comfortable with either outcome. I either refresh myself and bring about a neutral, objective mindset, or I further the process of education and understanding of the markets. Both of these alternatives are more appealing to me than getting desperate and gambling the market.

If I return to trading after performing these exercises and lose money on the next trade, I hang it up for the day. These are not days that I understand. I spend the rest of the day paper trading, and then analyze my results after the closing bell. For me, this is one of the best ways to figure out what it was that I didn't understand and what it was that cost me money. If you can continuously learn from your mistakes without costing yourself too much of what I call "tuition money," you will become a better, more successful trader over time.

Patience is a chromosome that I was not born with. It was something that I had to beat into my thick skull with a very large club. This chromosome (or lack thereof) has cost me quite a bit of money. I am aggressive and act on intuition in my day-to-day life. This spills over into my trading strategies, and I have to work very hard to control this impulse that I was born with. The aforementioned exercises have helped me quite a bit. However, I am still overcome by aggressiveness and impulsiveness from time to time. When I don't catch it, I usually lose money. After the fact, when I analyze my trades, I always realize when this character trait has reared its ugly head. As an exercise, I take a clean sheet of blank paper and write, "I will not be impulsive and irrational when I trade" 10 times. It sounds like something that my second grade teacher used to make me do when I pulled girls' hair on the playground. However, that exercise worked (I no longer pull hair), so I figure that this exercise is a good one to keep and use. Again, do what works for you.

Discipline is something that I have a great deal of in my life. This was not always the case, but something that I learned through athletics. I ran cross-country, participated in track and field events, was a hockey goaltender, rowed crew, and was a competitive freestyle mogul skier. Each of these physical activities yielded a different aspect of discipline in my life. Repetitive training was the key to my relative success in the sports that I participated in. The less I trained in an event/sport, the less I succeeded. The more I trained in an event/sport, the more I succeeded. I learned that nearly anything is possible with enough time, patience, practice, and, most importantly, discipline. If you set rules and guidelines to follow in both your active trading and your research of the markets, you will progress much faster than you would without a plan of action. Be patient. Don't give up. If at first you don't succeed, try, try again. If, after a reasonable period of time, you still don't succeed, quit.

Just kidding. Adjust your rules and guidelines, and try, try again. However, give yourself the luxury of time to determine if your strategy has the potential for success. If you are too quick to give up, you will inevitably pass up some incredible strategies and waste a considerable amount of time jumping around in the process.

In terms of active trading, you will always lose your discipline from time to time. It doesn't matter how experienced you are as a trader, it happens to everyone. If you are feeling desperate and begin to gamble or take pot shots at different stocks, STOP. Do whatever exercise you do to bring yourself back around. It is when you lose your discipline that you will yield your greatest losses and experience your greatest frustrations.

There is always tomorrow...unless you lose all of your money today. Then tomorrow consists of the want ads. Don't be afraid to give up on a trading day. Giving up on a trading day is not failure. It is healthy. It is something that great traders do when they know they are not in the right mindset or do not understand the current market conditions.

Giving up on a trading day is not failure. It is healthy.
Giving up on a trading day is not failure. It is healthy.
Giving up on a trading day is not failure. It is healthy.
Giving up on a trading day is not failure. It is healthy.
Giving up on a trading day is not failure. It is healthy.
Giving up on a trading day is not failure. It is healthy.

Giving up on a trading day is not failure. It is healthy.
Giving up on a trading day is not failure. It is healthy.
Giving up on a trading day is not failure. It is healthy.
Giving up on a trading day is not failure. It is healthy.

There, I feel better already. One note on this exercise: the copy and paste function on your word processor is not nearly as effective as good old-fashioned handwriting. If you cut corners and cheat, you are cheating no one but yourself. If you want to make money and be successful, don't cheat yourself. It's not healthy, and it doesn't work.

I will end this chapter on a personal note. On August 18, 1997, the day before a key Federal Reserve meeting in which the jury was still out on whether or not the Fed would raise interest rates, I entered the trading day with a very bearish bias.

Almost a year earlier, to the day, the market corrected. The planets were aligned in a strikingly similar formation, and I was certain that history would repeat itself on this day. I sold short a large position at the open and held it through the morning. The market was choppy, and, although the loss in my position was more than I am typically comfortable with, I was very bearish and disliked the market even more than I did at the open. I broke my most cherished trading rule and added to a losing position.

The market went against me again, but at this point, I was certain that the rally was fake and added to the position again. I was calm and comfortable with my position and truly felt that IBM was going to cave in at any moment. As the position continued against me....100 1/2, 101, 102, I started getting nervous. However, I had seen this alignment of the planets before and paid no attention to the FACT that the Ticks were strongly positive, and the futures as well as the Dow Industrial Average were both acting very bullish.

My loss going into the afternoon was sizeable, and I was pissed off at the market for not doing what it was "supposed" to do when it was "supposed" to do it. However, I anticipated that no one wanted to hold large positions overnight, the eve before a critical Fed meeting. I held my ground and didn't waver from my convictions. I ignored the numbers, which are facts, not opinions. When the Ticks are positive 642, the Ticks are positive 642. There is no interpretation that can dispel or discredit this fact. Nonetheless, I ignored the facts and substantiated my current position with a plethora of rationales.

Needless to say, IBM finished the day over 104, and I cashed out at a loss of approximately 25 percent of my trading capital. I spent the next few days not trading, but rather reviewing the day's events. I looked for indicators that would have alerted me that I should have reversed my position. I didn't see any while I was trading that day. In retrospect, the reason that I didn't see any contrary indicators was because I refused to look. Positively correlated stocks were acting bullish all day long. The Ticks, the Dow, the S&P, the Russell 2000, and the Nasdaq Composite index were acting bullish all day long. Regardless of the numbers, I refused to listen.

I broke my most sacred trading rule:
     NEVER ADD TO LARGE LOSING POSITIONS.
I broke my second most sacred trading rule:
     CUT YOUR LOSSES.

I broke my third most sacred trading rule:
   STAY OBJECTIVE.
I broke my fourth most sacred trading rule:
   ADMIT WHEN YOU ARE WRONG.
I broke my fifth most sacred trading rule:
   NEVER EXCEED A LOSS OF GREATER THAN
   10 PERCENT OF YOUR TRADING CAPITAL.

I lost discipline. I lost focus. I gambled. I took more risk than I should have taken. I lost my objectivity. This cost me huge and rattled me to the core. I lost self-esteem and was thoroughly discouraged. I was, however, smart enough to learn from the "tuition money." I took Tuesday, Wednesday, and Thursday off to reflect and study. I traded lightly on Friday and was back to my usual self the following Monday — a smarter, more disciplined, more careful, more objective trader than I was before.

The moral of this story is that what at first appears to be a terrible thing sometimes turns out to be a blessing in disguise. For me, August 18, 1997 was one of the greatest days of my life (in retrospect). I learned more about trading and psychology from that one day than the sum total of all of the previous trading experiences that I have had.

Losing trades are nothing more than the cost of tuition. The difference is that the bills are often much higher, and they come unexpectedly. If you can maintain a positive outlook on all of your trading experiences, and truly learn from your mistakes, the price paid for your education will be well spent.

ABOUT THE AUTHOR

When I was 16, I saw the movie "Wall Street." This was my first introduction to the financial markets. Before seeing this movie, I had no idea what I wanted to do with my life. After seeing this movie, I knew that I wanted to pursue a career in the financial markets. I began researching the markets, applied to business schools, and chose to attend Lehigh University.

After graduating from Lehigh with a Bachelor of Science Degree in Finance, I took a job as a financial analyst for a bank in Baltimore, Maryland. My goal was to learn as much about as many companies as possible and then take my experience to New York City and become a professional trader. It was during my tenure as an analyst that I began trading options. I was quite the loser at first, but as I read and learned more about the markets, I began to make money. The more I traded, the more I yearned to be a professional trader, and I eventually decided that it was time to move to Manhattan.

I took a job with Lehman Brothers, where I was involved in Municipal Bond trading. Over time, I realized that Municipal Bonds were not my forte and soon moved on. I spent some time consulting for various investment banks and eventually took a job with a Wall Street hedge fund. At this hedge fund I continued to trade options and began DayTrading stocks.

In October of 1997, I hung up my trading hat for a while and decided to help build an on-line DayTrading broker dealer in Texas. I spent nearly a year ramping up the business, and then returned to trading after a much deserved, extended vacation.

APPENDIX A: LISTED TRADING

For those DayTraders who don't yet have a background in listed trading, here is a summary for you. The information herein was compiled in 1997. Rules are subject to change, so you should contact your broker for a complete description of current rules and procedures.

The New York Stock Exchange Floor: Layout and Participants

The NYSE trading floor consists of four large adjoining rooms: the Garage, the Main Room, the Blue Room, and the Extended Blue Room. In the interior of the trading floor there are 17 trading posts. All trading in a given stock is centralized around one of these posts and its panel location. There are a total of 340 trading post panels, with each post having 18 or 22 panels. An average of eight issues are listed at each panel. On these panels are:

- The stock's ticker symbol
- The stock's last trade price
- How much the stock is up or down for the day
- The stock's inside bid and ask

- The amount of stock being bid for and offered at the bid ask
- The size of the last trade

It is at these posts that a trader known as the specialist works with his clerks to maintain an orderly trading market in the stocks that are assigned to him. The specialist always remains at the post while other traders, known as floor brokers, may go from post to post and may represent orders in all securities. Against the walls of the floor are floor broker booths occupied by floor broker clerks. The booths serve as a communications link between floor brokers and their firms and customers. Floor officials are employees of the NYSE and are readily accessible if they are needed to settle a dispute or to approve certain unusual transactions. Specialists and floor brokers are members of the NYSE.[5] Clerks are employees of the specialists and floor brokers.

Order Transmission and Execution

An order represents intent to buy or sell. Market orders request execution at the most advantageous price attainable after the order is represented in the "trading crowd." Limit orders request execution at a specified price or better, they will be filled only if that price is reached. In addition to these basic types of orders, there are several order types specifying further conditions for execution (sell plus, buy minus, good 'til canceled, stop orders, and market on close orders). Orders can also be divided into member orders (for the member's own account) or public orders (submitted by a member firm on behalf of a nonmember such as a retail client).

Orders originating off the floor of the Exchange reach the post and panel location where the stock is traded either electronically through the NYSE SuperDot system or is walked to the post by floor brokers. A recent study found that about 75 percent of orders reached the specialists via SuperDot. These orders, however, accounted for only 28 percent of executed NYSE share volume.[6] Floor brokers, therefore, tend to represent larger, more difficult-to-execute orders.

Floor brokers typically receive orders as follows: a member firm's trading desk telephones large own-account and institutional orders to the firm's floor booth. The booth personnel contact the floor broker,[7] who walks the order to the post where it is traded. Once at the post, the floor broker either leaves the order with the specialist or joins the trading crowd and bids for (or offers) the stock on behalf of his customer. Using floor brokers to transmit orders is difficult, so this method is generally used only for orders that require special care. The most common instance involves large orders that must be "worked" (exposed to the market bit by bit over time so as not to cause the price to jump too quickly in one direction), or large trades that are being "crossed." [8]

SuperDot orders come in from member firm trading desks over data communication lines that feed into the Exchange's Common Message Switch (CMS). Orders pass through CMS to the SuperDot, which processes and forwards them to the Post Support System (PSS). PSS then routes the orders to the specialist post. At the post, orders appear on the specialist Display Book screen.

The Display Book is an electronic workstation that keeps track of all limit orders and incoming market orders. The Display Book screen typically shows the near-the-market portion of the limit order book for each issue handled by the specialist.

Incoming SuperDot limit orders automatically enter the Display Book. The Display Book sorts the limit orders and displays them in price and time priority. When a floor broker gives the specialist a limit order, the specialist's clerk can enter the order into the Display Book using a keyboard. SuperDot market orders are displayed at the terminal and await action by the specialist. The specialist may execute a market order against another order in the Display Book, against his own inventory of stock, or against an order represented by a floor broker in the crowd. The order will be executed at or inside the displayed quote (the bid and ask), or the order may be "stopped" by the specialist.[9]

The message that an order has been executed (partially or completely) is called a report. The report goes from the specialist via PSS, SuperDot, and CMS to the traders who entered the orders involved in the trade. Even though the report is a formal notice that a trade has occurred, it is not publicly available and is not the same as the "print" of the transaction that appears on the Tape. The ultimate destination of the execution report is the investor who had placed the order. The path taken by the report is in most cases the reverse of the path that brought the order to the post in the first place.

Quote Reporting

Quote information disseminated by the Exchange consists of the highest NYSE bid and lowest NYSE offer price in every stock along with quote size (the minimum number of shares that can be bought or sold at this price). Quotes may represent the specialist's own trading interest, trading interest in the crowd, limit orders in the specialist's Display Book, or some combination. Irrespective of whose interest a quote represents, it is the specialist's responsibility to ensure that trades take place at prices no worse than the given quotes.

The NYSE requires that the specialist honor any request by a member to post a proprietary or agency "quote-improving" limit order. (A quote improvement is a quote posted inside the current spread. For example: if the current spread is 20 bid for 30,000 shares, 20,000 shares offered at 20 1/4, a quote-improving bid would be someone coming in with a bid of 20 1/8. This would be considered an improvement because the quote has narrowed.) On March 30, 1993, the NYSE issued a memo stating that all quote-improving limit orders arriving on the SuperDot implicitly dictate that they would like to create a price improvement. The specialist must update the quote on that particular stock as soon as possible in order to reflect the price improvement. A floor broker, however, has the right to request from the specialist that his inside-the-quote order not create a price improvement.

As far as market orders go, the specialist must expose them to the crowd and does not execute them automatically against the posted quote. Therefore, room is left for a price improvement where a market order will be executed at better than the quoted price and limit orders may be executed at better than the limit price.

For example, ABC is quoted at 20 bid for 30,000 shares, 20,000 shares offered at 95 1/4. Floor Broker A bids 95 1/8 for 5,000. Floor Broker B "hits the bid," and the two brokers complete the transaction at 95 1/8. Floor Broker A got a price improvement; instead of buying the stock at 95 1/4 (the posted offer) he bought at 95 1/8. The reasons that floor Broker B may have wanted to hit the bid may vary. For example, he may know that there is a very large seller of stock in the crowd and if he waits to execute his sale at 95 1/4 he may not get filled before the stock loses a lot of ground. He therefore opts to get rid of his stock at slightly less than the offer price in order to prevent this.

New York Stock Exchange Rule 123B

SuperDot provides the specialist with detailed real-time order-flow information. Aside from the obvious features of the order necessary to execute it properly (ticker symbol, buy or sell, market or limit, size, etc.), SuperDot orders also contain other identifying fields which the specialist may view on the Display Book, such as the entering firm's mnemonic, branch, and sequence number.

T'he NYSE prohibits specialists from disclosing to any person other than Exchange officials any information with regard to the orders entrusted to them. In 1991 this rule was amended to allow the specialist to reveal more information. It now allows the specialist to provide inquiring members with "information about buying or selling interest in the market at or near the prevailing quotation ... provided that the specialist shall make the same information available in a fair and impartial manner to any member whom shall so inquire." There is no way, however, for off-floor trading participants to obtain such information. This situation clearly creates an advantage to trading on the floor of the Exchange, as opposed to trading off it.

Priority, Parity, and Precedence: How it affects an order's standing

Priority: The first bidder at the best price gets as much of the first offer at that price for which he has bid. Time priorities go no further than this. If the first bidder does not fill his entire bid from the first offer, he has no prior claim on successive offers. The primary fact to remember is that the bid (or offer) that is entered first gets the first execution if the next sale is at that price.

Parity: When a sale takes place, all orders are cleared from the floor and must be re-entered to have standing in the next auction. From a practical standpoint, the remaining orders are considered re-entered simultaneously by the exchange's automated system. Parity in the NYSE auction means an equality of bids (or offers) at a given price. In other words, it is an absence of any clear preference or sequence of orders. Precedence based on size breaks parity.

Precedence: Precedence on size may occur in both parity and a priority situation after the priority bid or offer has been filled and a balance remains unfilled. There are two precedence-on-size situations: when individual bids either equal or exceed the amount offered. All bids equaling or exceeding the number of shares offered may compete for the stock. If there is a clear time sequence among these bidders, the stock is distributed according to time priority measured from last sale. When all individual bids are smaller than the amount offered, the largest bid gets first execution. If there are two or more bids of the same size, their equality is broken by time priority.[10]

Stopped Orders

In general, an incoming market order is exposed to the crowd to provide for a price improvement. Once exposed, the specialist will execute the order at the improved price in the crowd against the posted quote, or the specialist may "stop" the order. By stopping a market order, the specialist guarantees execution at the stop price (the current quote) while attempting to execute the order at a better price for an improvement. A stopped order, therefore, can be described as a guarantee-or-better order and is different from a stop order or a stop limit order.[11] Recent studies have shown that 26 percent of post-opening orders were stopped, and 62 percent of these stopped orders were executed at a price better than the stopped price.[12]

NYSE rules distinguish between stopping orders in a thinly spread market (1/8 or less) and stopping orders when the quoted spread is wider. In stocks whose spreads are 1/4 point or more, when the specialist is more likely to stop an order, the specialist should narrow the quotation spread by making a bid or an offer on behalf of the order that is being stopped.

For example, ABC is quoted 30 bid for 1,000 shares, 20,000 shares offered at 30 1/4. The specialist receives a market order to buy 500 shares. If not stopped, the order would be executed at 30 1/4, the prevailing offer. The specialist stops the order, guaranteeing that the order will receive no worse than 30 1/4. The specialist then bids 30 1/8 on behalf of the stopped order. ABC is now quoted at 30 1/8 bid for 500 shares, 20,000 shares offered at 30 1/4. If one of the sellers hits the 30 1/8 bid, the buyer received a price improvement by having his order stopped (he bought at 30 1/8 instead of 30 1/4).

A stop order to buy (sell) becomes a market order when a transaction in the security occurs at or above (below) the stop price after the order is represented in the crowd. A stop limit order to buy (sell) becomes a limit order executable at the limit price or better when a transaction in the security occurs at or above (below) the stop price.

In minimum variation markets (this formerly meant 1/8, but since July 1997 the minimum variation on the NYSE has been 1/16) the specialist may stop market orders of 2,000 shares or less. The Exchange prohibits the specialist from stopping orders routinely in minimum variation markets.

According to the NYSE, "an order should be stopped in such a market only in situations in which there is an imbalance on the opposite side of the market from the order being stopped, and the imbalance is of sufficient size, given the characteristics of the security, to suggest the likelihood of price improvement."[13]

In stopping an order in a minimum variation market, the specialist should change the quoted bid or offer size to reflect the size of the order being stopped. The stopped order goes behind, in terms of time priority, any limit orders already on the specialist's book at the quote, but will be executed before any of the specialist's own interest in at that price.

For example, ABC is quoted at 30 bid for 1000 shares, 20,000 shares offered at 30 1/8. The large imbalance on the offer side suggests that a buy market order, if stopped, is likely to receive a price improvement. If the specialist receives a market order to buy 500 shares, and the order is not stopped, it will be filled at 30 1/8, the prevailing offer. The specialist stops the order, guaranteeing that the order will receive no worse than 30 1/8, and adds the order to the other 30, creating a new quote of 30 bid for 1,500 shares, 20,000 shares offered at 30 1/8. The 1,000 shares already at the bid have time priority over the stopped 500 shares.

The practice of stopping market orders help to maintain an orderly market and are one of the methods used by the specialist in maintaining a size balance between the quoted bid and ask. Stopping stock can also help reduce short-run price reversals. In quarter-point markets, for example, a series of rapidly arriving buy and sell market orders would, in the absence of any stops, result in a sequence of transactions at successive 1/4 point variations. In such situations, stopping market orders would result in most transactions being executed inside the quote, benefiting both the buy and sell market orders.

Crossing Orders

A broker will occasionally bring to the floor orders representing both the buy and sell side of a transaction with the intention of crossing them. This may happen when the broker's trading desk has received separate buy and sell orders in the same stock from two different customers. The NYSE prohibits, with certain exemptions, member firms from executing proprietary and in-house trades in NYSE listed stocks off an organized exchange.[14] The prohibition, however, only applies to cases in which the firm represents both sides of the off-market cross. If two separate member firms wish to execute a trade with each other off an organized exchange, they may do so.

The NYSE also requires that a broker, before proceeding with a cross, must make a public bid and offer on behalf of both sides of the cross. This rule was established to allow other brokers to match the stock bid for or offered by the broker who would like to cross. When a broker does, in fact, put up a bid and ask with intention to cross, he may do so with a minimum variation spread. Orders may therefore be crossed at or inside the prevailing quote. Orders of 10,000 shares or more ("blocks") may be crossed outside the prevailing quote.[15] However, when a broker wants to cross an order, he is required to bring both sides of the stock to the trading crowd. He must also observe the market's principles of bid and offer parity and precedence.

For example, ABC is quoted 20 bid for 2,000 shares, 3,000 shares offered at 20 1/8. A broker wants to cross 5,000 shares at 20 1/8, so he must bid 20 for 5,000 shares and offer 5,000 shares at 20 1/8. The 2,000 shares at the bid and the 3,000 shares at the offer have time priority over the crossing brokers bid and offer. In order to get around this problem of priority, the broker may do as follows: he may buy (on behalf of the buy side of the cross) 100 shares from the 3,000 shares offered at 20 1/8. This trade effectively places the crossing broker's offer at 20 1/8 on parity, as far as time preference is concerned, with all other offers at 20 1/8. The broker may now proceed and cross the remaining 4,900 shares, claiming precedence based on size ("sizing out" smaller orders at the quote) and take his own 4,900 shares offered at 20 1/8.

The crossing of blocks outside the prevailing quotes is governed by the NYSE. The Exchange formally defines blocks as trades of either 10,000 shares or $200,000, whichever is less. Under NYSE Rules[16], a member receiving a block order which may not be readily absorbed by the market should first explore interest in the crowd, including the specialist's own interest. If asked, the specialist may recommend a "clean-up" price for the block. A member wanting to cross a block of stock at a specific price outside the quote must announce a clean-up price to the crowd and then may follow one of two procedures. In the first procedure the member must fill, at the announced clean-up price, all orders in the book and in the crowd as well as all better-priced displayed Intermarket Trading System (ITS) quotes. (ITS is an electronic communications network that links market professionals from the major listed exchanges.)

For example, the prevailing offer for ABC is 5,000 shares at 20 1/4, another 2,000 shares offered at 20 3/8 and 1,000 shares more offered at 20 1/2. A broker announces a block cross of 30,000 shares at a clean-up price of 20 1/2. The specialist wants to sell 2,000 shares from his inventory at this price, and there is no other crowd or ITS interest. Under the first procedure, the broker must buy the 5,000 shares from the quoted offer of 20 1/4, the 2,000 offered at 20 3/8, the 1,000 offered at 20 1/2, and the 2,000 offered by the specialist all at 20 1/2. The offers at 20 1/4 and 20 3/8 get the benefit of the clean-up price, even though they were offers to sell at a lower price, and the block trader is only able to cross the amount of stock for which there was no other floor interest.

If a broker feels that under the first procedure he will give away an excessive portion of his cross, an alternative procedure can be used. The broker can inform the crowd that he will not give them stock at the cleanup price. The broker then makes a public bid and offer on behalf of both sides of the cross (with a minimum variation spread) and allows a reasonable time for the crowd and the specialist to trade. After the crowd and specialist trade, the crossing broker can cross the orders for the remaining shares at the clean-up price. Even according to this procedure, however, the crossing broker must fill all the limit orders in the book that are at the cross price before retaining any stock for his own account.

Market vs. Limit Orders

In markets where traders may enter different types of orders, the choice of order submission is one of the most crucial the trader will make. Traders must typically decide when to use a market order and when to use a limit order. These are by far the two most common orders entered on the NYSE. Market orders pay an implicit price for immediacy while limit orders bear the risk of non-execution.

A trader's order submission strategy depends on the trading problem that he faces; therefore, evaluation of order execution performance must take this into account. For example, a trader who needs to quickly liquidate a position may be willing to pay for immediacy. This trader, who is pre-committed to trading, will probably choose to use a market order to trade. On the other hand, a trader who is only interested in making a profitable round trip (DayTrading) and who has no fundamental reason to establish a position, will not pay for liquidity. Instead, this trader is likely to offer limit orders and hope that other traders who do demand immediacy will take his offer. He is a passive trader in the sense that he will only trade if someone else initiates.

When deciding what type of order to enter, the trader must also take into consideration the prevailing spread in the stock he plans to buy or sell, and how many shares his order is going to be. In a study done by Lawrence Harris and Joel Hasbrouck[17], they found that for orders under 200 shares, market orders tend to do better than the prevailing quote (the offer for a buy order and the bid for a sell order) that exists at the time the order is entered by 1.73 cents/share in 1/8 point spread markets, by 8.24 cents/share in 1/4 markets, and 11.14 cents/share in 3/8 markets. Clearly, the price improvement received increases as the prevailing spread widens. When market orders are of larger size, however, the overall price improvements decrease dramatically. For 1,000 share market orders in 1/8, 1/4, and 3/8 markets, the price improvements are -.09 cents/share, 3.84 cents/share, and 2.51 cents/share, respectively.

When considering a limit order, another dimension is added to the trader's decision: the choice of how far away from the prevailing quote to enter the order. In their study, Hasbrouck and Harris found that this decision (along with the size of the order and the width of the prevailing spread) can determine how much better or worse the trader's order will be executed away from the quote that existed at the time of the order's entry.

In 1/8 markets, 200-share orders entered with at-the-quote limit orders received a 4.76 cents/share improvement and a 1.18 cents/share improvement when entered at 1/8 better than the quote. Similarly, 1,000 share orders did slightly better in 1/8 markets with at the quote orders more than 1/8 better than the quote orders. As the market spreads grow, however, so does the benefit of entering better than the market limits, as opposed to at the quote orders. In 1/4 markets, 200 share orders received 8.02 cents/share improvements with at the quote orders and 10.20 cents/share improvements with 1/8 better than the quote orders. One-thousand share orders received 5.25 cents/share improvements with 1/8 better than the quote orders.

A number of very important observations can be made from this statistical study:

- Market orders frequently better the prevailing counterpart quote.
- In 1/8 point markets, at-the-quote limit orders achieve better average performance than do market orders, although at the cost of higher variability of execution.
- In 1/4 point and 3/8 point markets, placing limit orders at the quote is an inferior strategy. Limit orders that better the quote by 1/8 in 1/4 point markets, and by 1/8 or 1/4 in 3/8 point markets, appear to perform well.

The quoted study was performed before the NYSE switched over to minimum variation spreads of 1/16, which may alter the average price improvement received for particular orders. The significance of the trader's choice of order entry, however, and the conditions under which he does so, can still clearly be seen.

In another study on market orders by Ross, Shapiro, and Smith[18], the authors conclude that price improvements of market orders in 1/8 point markets (then the minimum variation market) are not so uncommon, as might have been previously thought. They found that about 40 percent of market orders in such cases received price improvements. They also found that price improvements are much more common in more actively traded stocks, and that most improvements (73 percent) were from interaction of market orders with other orders, not the specialist.

Odd-lot Orders

Stocks are typically traded in "round-lot" units of 100 shares. Odd-lot orders are those that are comprised of orders less than 100 shares. Odd-lots are executed automatically against the specialist's inventory. Odd-lot market orders are executed automatically upon receipt at the best ITS quote. Odd-lot limit orders are executed at the limit price or better immediately following a round-lot NYSE trade at that price, again, against the specialist's own inventory. Odd-lot orders are not disseminated on the Tape.

The specialist learns of odd-lot orders via an odd-lot advisory (OLA). A single OLA will generally cover many transactions. At the end of the day, the specialist is notified of the prices at which individual odd-lot transactions occurred.

Member firms are not allowed to combine the odd-lot orders given by several different customers into round-lot orders without getting customer approval for "bunching" their order. At the same time, to limit the possibility of abuse of the automated odd-lot trading system (which automatically fills the trade against the specialist's inventory), a broker dealer entering multiple odd-lot orders for the same account in the same stock is required to aggregate the orders into round-lots, where possible, for execution in the round-lot auction market.

Specialist Trading

The trades of the specialists on the NYSE are crucial to the existence of the Exchange as a "dealer market." The purpose of the specialists, according to the Exchange, is to keep a fair and orderly market in the stocks assigned to them. The necessity for the specialist to be involved in the trading, however, varies greatly from stock to stock. In a recent study[19] it was shown that in certain stocks (seven percent of the sampled stocks) the specialist participation rate (the ratio of specialist share purchases and sales to total reported share volume) exceeds 60 percent. These stocks essentially trade in "dealer markets," with the specialist taking the opposite side of virtually all transactions. At the other extreme, the study found that in certain stocks (17 percent of the sampled stocks), the specialist participation rate in trades is less than 10 percent. These stocks trade in what approximates a pure "auction market" where investors trade with one another with minimal specialist dealer trading. The study also found that specialists participate less in large transactions, possibly because many large transactions reach the floor after upstairs trading desks have had the opportunity to solicit counter-party interest.

In another study[16] it was shown that specialists trade extensively inside the quoted spread: only 40 percent of specialist buy trades, for example, take place at the quoted bid; 37 percent occur at the quoted midpoint; and 22 percent occur at above the quoted midpoint. The average quoted spread prevailing whenever the specialist participates in a trade is 22 cents, but specialist earn only 7 cents per trade in "spread revenue." Clearly, therefore, specialists trade extensively within the quoted spread. The study also finds (similar to the study by Madhaven and Soflanos) that specialist participation rate in total trade volume ranges from 42 percent for the 251 least active stocks to 15 percent for the 251 most actively traded stocks. This finding reaffirms the specialist's function as that of a "liquidity supplier of last resort" whose presence is lacking in over the counter markets.

Unusual Market Conditions

When the level of trading activity in a stock is such that the Exchange cannot collect, process, and disseminate quotes accurately, the specialist, with Floor Official approval, may switch to "non-firm-mode" for 30 minutes. When in the non-firm mode, it may not be possible for transactions to be executed at the disseminated quotes. Specialists may extend the non-firm mode beyond 30 minutes following a review by Floor Officials.

In unusual market conditions the specialist, with Floor Official approval, may delay the opening of a stock or temporarily halt trading. There are three primary reasons for opening delays and trading halts: large order imbalances, news pending, and news dissemination. Trading may be temporarily suspended to allow time to evaluate news and to attract counter-balancing interest. In each case a message is disseminated on the Tape.

"News pending" refers to cases where listed companies are about to make announcements that may have substantial market impact. When a company plans to make such announcements, the Exchange recommends that the company notify the Exchange at least 10 minutes prior to the announcement. Listed companies may also make an outright request that trading in their stock be halted. Such a request, however, does not guarantee that a halt will occur. The Exchange will inform a Floor Official of the impending news and/or trading halt request, and the Floor Official will decide whether trading should be halted.

Trading halts due to order imbalances are considered "non-regulatory," which means that regional exchanges may continue to trade and that all trade information is disseminated to the Tape. "News pending" and "news dissemination" trading halts are considered "regulatory," and the regional Exchanges will follow the NYSE's lead and also halt trading.

During opening delays and trading halts, quote indications will usually be disseminated to the Tape. Quote indications attempt to signal market indications and the likely reopening price in order to attract counter balancing interest in the stock. The dissemination of an indication is mandatory for any opening that will result in a price significantly different from the previous NYSE close. An indication should also be published immediately when trading is halted for a non-regulatory order imbalance and prior to the reopening of a stock following a trading halt or opening delay. Any stock that is not opened with a trade or reasonable quotation within 30 minutes after the start of the trading day is considered a delayed opening and requires the supervision of a Floor Official.

APPENDIX B: ENDNOTES

[1] LibertyLifewebsite,http://www.liberty.co.za/gloss/sae00169.htm.

[2] Equis web site, http://www.equis.com/customer/formulas/cf00003.html.

[3] W. Stansbury Carnes, Stephen D. Slifer, *The Atlas of Economic Indicators* (Harper Collins Publishers, 1991).

[4] David Lieberman, "Intraday Trading Procedures on The New York Stock Exchange." Senior thesis, 1997.

[5] NYSE membership is vested with the individual trader and not with a firm. The individual members can, however, enable their firms to qualify for membership.

[6] Joel Hasbrouck, George Sofianos, Deborah Sosbee "New York Stock Exchange Systems and Trading Procedures," New York Stock Exchange Working Paper #93-01. The number is calculated as follows: total executed SuperDot orders divided by twice the total share volume. A 1,000-share trade, for example, may consist of a 1,000-share sell SuperDot order and 1,000-share buy order in the crowd. The SuperDot share of this trade is 50 percent.

[7] Until recently the floor broker would be in contact with his booth by using one of the strategically placed yellow telephones that stand near the posts. Today, however, many floor brokers use special in-house cellular phones to contact their booth, which saves them time and also makes it much easier for the booth to contact them.

contact their booth, which saves them time and also makes it much easier for the booth to contact them.

[8] See Crossing Orders section in Appendix A.

[9] See Stopped Orders section in Appendix A.

[10] ABN AMRO listed trading pamphlet, 1997.

[11] A stop order to buy (sell) becomes a market order when a transaction in the security occurs at or above (below) the stop price after the order is represented into the crowd. A stop limit order to buy (sell) becomes a limit order executable at the limit price or better when a transaction in the security occurs at or above (below) the stop price.

[12] Joel Hasbrouck, George Sofianos, Deborah Sosbee, "New York Stock Exchange Systems and Trading Procedures," New York Stock Exchange Working Paper # 93-01.

[13] New York Stock Exchange Surveillance Memo, April 3, 1991.

[14] New York Stock Exchange Rule 390.

[15] New York Stock Exchange Rule 127.

[16] New York Stock Exchange Rule 127.

[17] Joel Hasbrouck, Lawrence Harris, "Market vs. Limit Orders: The SuperDot Evidence on Order Submission Strategy." New York Stock Exchange Working Paper # 92-02.

[18] Katherine D. Ross, James E. Shapiro, Katherine Smith, "Price Improvements of SuperDot Market Orders on the New York Stock Exchange." New York Stock Exchange Working Paper #96-02.

[19] Ananth Madhaven, George Sofianos, "Auction and Dealer Markets: An Empirical Analysis of New York Stock Exchange Specialist Trading." New York Stock Exchange Working Paper # 94-01.

[20] George Sofianos, "Specialist Gross Trading Revenues at the New York Stock Exchange." New York Stock Exchange Working Paper # 95-01.

NOTES

<u>NOTES</u>

<u>NOTES</u>

NOTES

NOTES

NOTES